Advance Pr

"Burnout is not a personal failing—it's a call to reimagine how we care for ourselves and each other. In *8 Keys to Healing, Managing, and Preventing Burnout*, Morgan Johnson blends science, storytelling, and practical tools to support anyone feeling stuck in cycles of exhaustion. With humor, heart, and empathy, this book offers a pathway to healing that feels both achievable and deeply human."
—**Silvy Khoucasian, MA,** relationship coach, founder of *Love With Integrity* podcast, and author of the *12 Months of Self-Discovery* journal

"As a therapist who has experienced significant periods of burnout, Morgan Johnson's *8 Keys to Healing, Managing, and Preventing Burnout* is a necessary addition to the burnout canon. With the perfect blend of research, personal experience, and her work aiding clients, this book is essential not just for helping professionals, but, as Johnson says, for anyone who is human. This book not only updates us on burnout research and different ways of considering this issue, it updates us on how to effectively move through burnout when we are in it and how to prevent it in the future."
—**Ilyse Kennedy, LPC-S, LMFT-S,** author of *The Tender Parts: A Guide to Healing Trauma Through Internal Family Systems Therapy*

"Morgan Johnson is a dynamic teacher who embodies the wisdom she teaches, and reading *8 Keys to Healing, Managing, and Preventing Burnout* is like getting to take one of her sought-after classes. Johnson offers readers practical tips and a caring companion through the ups and downs of fulfilling our vocations; she is a trusted guide for both new and seasoned practitioners."
—**Gena St. David, PhD,** professor of counselor education at Seminary of the Southwest and author of *The Brain and the Spirit*

"As an emergency physician who has suffered and recovered from extreme burnout, it is my sincere opinion that for medical professionals, reading *8 Keys to Healing, Managing, and Preventing Burnout* is the literary equivalent of putting your oxygen mask on first before assisting other passengers."
—**J. Mack Slaughter, MD,** emergency medicine attending physician, founder of Music Meets Medicine, content creator

8 KEYS TO HEALING, MANAGING, AND PREVENTING BURNOUT

8 Keys to Mental Health Series
Babette Rothschild, Series Editor

The 8 Keys series of books provides consumers with brief, inexpensive, and high-quality self-help books on a variety of topics in mental health. Each volume is written by an expert in the field, someone who is capable of presenting evidence-based information in a concise and clear way. These books stand out by offering consumers cutting-edge, relevant theory in easily digestible portions, written in an accessible style. The tone is respectful of the reader and the messages are immediately applicable. Filled with exercises and practical strategies, these books empower readers to help themselves.

8 KEYS TO HEALING, MANAGING, AND PREVENTING BURNOUT

MORGAN JOHNSON

FOREWORD BY
BABETTE ROTHSCHILD

Norton Professional Books
An Imprint of W. W. Norton & Company
Independent Publishers Since 1923

Note to Readers: This book is intended as a general information resource for professionals practicing in the field of psychotherapy and mental health. It is not a substitute for appropriate training or clinical supervision. Standards of clinical practice and protocol vary in different practice settings and change over time. No technique or recommendation is guaranteed to be safe or effective in all circumstances, and neither the publisher nor the author can guarantee the complete accuracy, efficacy, or appropriateness of any particular recommendation in every respect or in all settings or circumstances.

Any URLs displayed in this book link or refer to websites that existed as of press time. The publisher is not responsible for, and should not be deemed to endorse or recommend, any website other than its own or any content that it did not create. The author, also, is not responsible for any third-party material.

Copyright © 2025 by Morgan Johnson

All rights reserved
Printed in the United States of America
First Edition

For information about permission to reproduce selections from this book, write to Permissions, W. W. Norton & Company, Inc., 500 Fifth Avenue, New York, NY 10110

For information about special discounts for bulk purchases, please contact W. W. Norton Special Sales at specialsales@wwnorton.com or 800-233-4830

Manufacturing by Versa Press
Book design by Daniel Lagin
Production manager: Gwen Cullen

ISBN: 978-1-324-05388-0

W. W. Norton & Company, Inc., 500 Fifth Avenue, New York, NY 10110
www.wwnorton.com

W. W. Norton & Company Ltd., 15 Carlisle Street, London W1D 3BS

1 2 3 4 5 6 7 8 9 0

*This book is dedicated to Leo the dog,
who made sure I laughed every day
for 12 wonderful years.*

Contents

Foreword by Babette Rothschild   xiii

Acknowledgments   xvii

Introduction   xix

KEY 1: Identify and Appreciate Your Own Social, Cultural, and Psychological Risks   3

KEY 2: Recognize When You Are Careening Toward Burnout   33

KEY 3: Learn When and How to Slow Down, Step Back, or Walk Away   59

KEY 4: Do Something With the Stress   79

KEY 5: Figure Out What Keeps Your Fire Going   99

KEY 6: Throw Your Hands Up Without Giving Up   119

KEY 7: Cultivate Healthy Pressure-Release Valves   135

KEY 8: Focus On Something *Bigger*   157

Wrapping Up: Carrying on in Community   175

Resources and Further Reading   179

References   181

Index   187

Foreword

The 8 Keys Series was conceived to provide a library of intelligent, highly accessible books to self-help readers who may not want or be able to afford psychotherapy. The series aims to provide those readers with readily applicable techniques to aid the recovery of the condition being discussed. Each series volume can be easily used as self-help or as an adjunct to psychotherapy. From a wealth of correspondence and other feedback, I know that my own book, *8 Keys to Safe Trauma Recovery*, the first in this series, along with the more recently published companion *8 Keys to Safe Trauma Recovery Workbook*, are being used in both of these ways. In addition, each book in the series includes theory portions which are most relevant to the featured topic to ensure that both the consumer and helping professional are similarly informed. Informed consumers make better decisions about what does and does not help them. It has always been my belief that any seeker of improved psychological health or personal growth should have access to the same information as the professionals; the theories and techniques that the psychotherapists learn and use should never be kept a secret. That is no less true in this volume, *8 Keys to Healing, Managing, and Preventing Burnout*. Among these pages you will find a wealth of information and tools that will help you to prevent or recover from burnout.

Burnout is universal: everyone is vulnerable to it and anyone can succumb to its effects. Of course, some situations and jobs carry a higher likelihood of burnout, but really, everybody is at risk. The longer the hours, the more intense the work and responsibility, the less chance for adequate time off, the less support, and so on, are just some of the factors that can put someone in jeopardy. Doctors and lawyers are among the most obvious categories of burnout candidates. However, parents, family caregivers, teachers, students, factory workers, social workers, psychotherapists, and others may be equally at risk.

When I began to train psychotherapists and body psychotherapists in theory, principles, and techniques of somatic trauma therapy in the mid 1990s, one of the first things I noticed among the professional participants was a high level of burnout. An astounding number of therapists came to my trainings with one foot already out the door of their workplaces, including public clinics and private practices. Despite the fact of loving their work, a large percentage were tempted to abandon their clients because they were exhausted and overburdened. As a group, generally, they were too easily impacted by hearing about the horrors that had happened to those they were hoping to help and feeling responsible for healing them. Clearly, something was wrong.

Just about everyone who aspires to help others wants and intends to be able to do that for a long and healthy career. Why else would they go to the expense, time, and effort to train and do that work? It would be an understatement to say I was surprised and concerned to find such a difficulty among my students! That led me to questioning what could be at play. At the time, I was living and working in Copenhagen, Denmark. My curiosity and concern drove me to spend many hours and days at the Copenhagen Nature and Medical Library digging into journals and interlibrary–loaned books (internet searching via Yahoo and Google was only just beginning in those days and online information was extremely limited). It was difficult to find anything helpful as the concept of burnout had only been recognized since the early 1970s (Samra, 2018).* My library research instead uncovered books, studies, and articles on stress management, empathy, and emotional contagion, eventually culminating in my own book specifically for helping professionals, *Help for the Helper* (2005).

In sync with the times, Morgan Johnson has taken on a much broader view of the reach of burnout, including the helping professions but also extending well beyond. She brings in a wider perspective on contributing factors including current events, business practices, and politics. Her knowledge and expertise are evident on every page. In addition, she is generous and patient in the tactics she suggests for managing and preventing burnout, making it possible for each reader to tailor interventions to their own needs. Morgan is also one of the most engaging authors I have worked with and read. Even when discussing difficult topics, she is warm, engaging, and fun to read, like having a lively conversation with an intimate and candid friend. For anyone in danger of or already suffering from burnout, *8 Keys to Healing, Managing, and Preventing Burnout* will prove a very valuable read.

—Babette Rothschild, MSW, LCSW

---

* Samra, R. (2018). Brief history of burnout. *The BMJ*. 363.

Acknowledgments

Enormous gratitude and appreciation first to Babette Rothschild. It is the honor of a lifetime to contribute to my favorite therapist's book series. I would not be the author or therapist I am without Babette's wisdom and incredible writing—she showed me that it's possible (and necessary) to bring both science and soul to process. Thanks also to my amazing Norton editor, Jamie Vincent. And always, thanks to every client and student who has trusted me with their story.

Introduction

When I began writing this book in 2023, one of my first, conscious goals was to write a book about burnout *without* burning out. After almost a decade of serving burnt-out clients as a psychotherapist (and burning out a few times myself along the way), I've learned you can't just talk the talk—you have to walk the walk. I'm thrilled to have the opportunity to provide some strategies for healing, managing, and preventing burnout. *Burnout* is not just about exhaustion; it has to do with how alive you feel inside, how intact—whole. Is there a fire inside keeping you energized? Or is the porch light on, but no one's home? The opposite of burnout is *thriving* and *flourishing*—it's feeling attuned and connected with the world around you, being able to fully absorb moments of joy, ease, pleasure, and peace.

Through my own personal experiences with burnout, I found myself continually offered empty reminders about self-care, and referrals to various yoga studios, wellness retreats, and life coaches. Have you ever felt interrogated when you mentioned how exhausted and burnt out you felt? Have you been bombarded with questions about whether you're practicing enough self-care, getting enough sleep, taking the right supplements, and engaging with the right breathing exercises or yoga postures? "Are you taking care of yourself?" is to burnout as "Sorry for your loss" is to grief. As benign as their intentions may be, many people just don't know how to respond to authentic expressions of hopelessness or the other intense emotions that tend to accompany burnout. Sometimes people are asking, "How are you?" simply because it's part of the social choreography they've been trained in—they don't want an honest response, just to stick to the script—it's not malicious. There's something insidious, though, about the apparent obsession with centering self-care in the frame while discussing relief and solutions.

Often when people ask about your self-care, what they really mean is, *If you were taking proper care of yourself, you wouldn't be suffering from burnout*—the (usually) unintentional implication is that you are the problem, that you are the one who should (or even could) be able to put a stop to your suffering. I notice this felt sense of judgment is an especially common experience for people who work in helping professions and other occupations that have historically been more male-dominated, like science and medicine. It's also common for students and trainees working toward licensure/certification (e.g., medical residency or clinical internship) to report trying to keep their burnout symptoms and treatment efforts incredibly private, especially if it has to do with mental health, because struggles with mental health and wellness are still too frequently seen as weakness.

As a therapist, one of my specializations is supporting health and helping professionals (e.g., surgeons, nurses, emergency department staff, social workers, other therapists) who are struggling with burnout. These people spend years and years studying human bodies. They know what needs to happen for proper care—often they even manage it for themselves pretty well. They are already paying attention to sleep hygiene. They are staying hydrated and nourished. Many are trying combinations of joyful movement and meditation. They are already sitting through the yearly "not mandatory" burnout workshop scheduled during lunch break (which is justified by including a pizza lunch). It's often through sobs that they give me the long list of everything they're already doing, everything they've already tried, to get some relief, only to conclude that nothing really seems to help. Under the weight of hopelessness, it gets easier to believe negative thoughts about yourself. *Of all people, with all your knowledge and training—after everything you fought to overcome—even you can't pull yourself out of this darkness? You should be able to pull yourself together!* This is how I'd distill the big struggle that comes up again and again for so many helpers.

A large part of solutions for burnout is sorting out how to work smarter, not harder. Sure, you may be asked to invest some energy and effort initially as you begin making your way through this book, but the idea is that as you increase your understanding and awareness, make some plans, and conduct a few mini-experiments, you can start feeling more ease, wholeness, and joy—less burnout. A few shifts, changes, and reframes are going to help make things feel easier, even if some of the learning and onboarding is effortful or challenging. Don't worry, I'm going to give you loads of practical tips that have worked for all sorts of people.

Another big part burnout relief is just acknowledging the fact that the game is rigged, as burnout researchers Emily Nagoski and Amelia Nagoski (2019) say. Our systems, to a large extent, have depended on exploitation, especially of marginalized and minoritized people. Without an appreciation for context, history, power, and oppression, you run the risk of blaming your burnout symptoms on yourself. You have to be able to recognize what's normal for our human family— including limitations!—so that when you're being expected to be super-human or robot-like, you can at least recognize and acknowledge the unfairness.

Singer-songwriter, podcast host, and author Michael Gungor (2012), says, "Burnout is what happens when you try to avoid being human for too long." Humans need to explore and play. We need to relax, rest, and sleep. We need to be able to dream and create, to connect and attune intimately with other humans. To the extent we are able, we need to move our bodies joyfully. We are feeling, connecting, meaning-making creatures. Intentionally doing these things gives messages of safety to the primitive parts of our bodies that don't speak a formal language—that can't be reassured by just hearing someone say, "Hey, don't worry, it's going to be okay." With human bodies it's more show than tell. It can be easy to forget that humans are a part of nature. But research shows that spending time in natural settings, such as hiking, going to the beach, swimming in a lake, even simply viewing some trees while outdoors, is one of the more efficient ways to calm your body and mind and help get your nervous system balanced and back to a comfortable baseline.

So how do I know that I've achieved my goal of writing this book without burning out? I know because I still feel human. I still feel . . . myself. Internally, energetically, I can sense a surplus, not a deficit, and things I love actually give me a noticeable lift. I want to connect with people I care about. I'm not content to show up as a smiling hollow shell. And this is absolutely by no means an "if I can do it, if my clients can do it, so can you!" statement. In fact, you'll hear a lot about *toxic positivity* and how it doesn't help. I offer plenty of different ways of thinking and practical tips to try. Sure, these are based on a lot of personal experience, both mine and clients'. But what I really want to offer you are possibilities—opportunities for feeling less overwhelmed, alone, and broken—because wherever you are, you deserve to feel whole, connected, and thriving.

WHO IS THIS BOOK FOR?

Who is most likely to experience burnout? One of the original researchers to study the phenomena of burnout, Herbert Freudenberger (1974) observed that it's "the dedicated and the committed" (p. 161). This book is meant for anyone dedicated and committed—whether that's because you fully love what you do or because you've got to keep showing up to pay the rent and care for those you love. This

INTRODUCTION   xxiii

is for anyone at their wit's end, feeling exhausted and exasperated and unsure where to begin, or feeling overwhelmed and trying to avoid burnout, whether you're taking care of your job responsibilities or taking care of people who need you.

You'll be most likely to benefit from this book if you are or suspect you are experiencing one or more of the following:

- Burnout from work (including education/training)
- Burnout from being a parent or caregiver
- Burnout from living with certain diagnoses and chronic conditions
- A combination of the above (e.g., burnout from working plus caregiving, or burnout from parenting and going through cancer treatment)

This book is also for people who aren't burning out but just want to know more—to prevent it in yourself, to make the workplace better for employees, to better understand and support someone you love who's burnt out, or even just to learn more about human bodies, minds, and relationships under stress and some practical, effective ways to cope. If you're in a leadership position, I hope to inspire you not only to care for yourself and your employees, but also to use your leadership to help create some of the big shifts and changes our world desperately needs.

HOW THIS BOOK IS ORGANIZED

This book offers eight unique keys for recovering from, managing, and preventing burnout. Each chapter zooms in on a different key, covering what's at issue and offering theory and background, and provides four activities to deepen and expand your understanding of the key. I share a mix of science, history, theory, therapy techniques, and skills, as well as personal anecdotes. Out of respect and to safeguard the privacy and confidentiality of clients I serve, I do not share client stories. I *do* offer some generalized descriptions from my work, where appropriate. My hope is that you take what you like from the book and leave the rest. If I make a recommendation that doesn't feel like it fits you, please skip it.

If you're burning or burnt out, the last thing you want is to feel like you're being pushed to do things out of alignment with your values and wants—to feel pushed *at all* can feel too much when you have already been pushing yourself to the brink. I also appreciate that it is possible you work in a job where you are actively, chronically enduring traumatization. You may have already developed PTSD before coming to the work you currently do—I appreciate the layers. And I promise you that I don't want to be another person making you feel uncomfortable, disempowered, or like it's "my way or the highway." At the end of each chapter, I invite you to (a) think through what felt helpful and unhelpful and (b) make a plan to implement, adapt, or pass on any of my recommendations.

Although it's likely that you will get the most out of this book if you move through the keys in numerical order, it's *okay* if you prefer to engage by flipping through and starting where you feel most curious. Each chapter introduces some research and psychoeducation and then builds on itself, so if you take the nonlinear approach but feel confused at any point, I invite you to skim back through the chapter introduction or theory section to see if you missed something foundational. I'm diagnosed with ADHD and can easily feel overwhelmed with big blocks of text. I also love to skip around! So, my hope is to present information in ways that are easily accessible to you regardless of how your brain works, or how exhausted you are. Some questions and activities require parts of your brain that you may not be able to fully access at the moment, if you are incredibly stressed out and exhausted—you'll often see invitations to save things for when you are more resourced and better equipped to engage.

A note on "Relational Activity Add-Ons": If you are in a relationship or regularly connect with someone, such as a partner, friend, or loved one, a colleague, coworker, or mentor, these "add-ons" at the end of activities are things you can do together, where appropriate, if the other person is interested. Some of your healing will occur in solitude, and some will happen through relationships and interpersonal experiences—my hope is to offer a range of accessible ways to recover from, manage, and prevent burnout.

WHAT DOES "BURNOUT RECOVERY" TYPICALLY INVOLVE?

Are you curious if recovering from or preventing burnout is really possible? Most burnt-out people I've encountered fall into one of three categories: (1) actively burnt to a crisp and in need of serious help; (2) treading water, but only just barely, and starting to notice a decline in engagement in important areas of life (e.g., job, family, friendships, hobbies); or (3) looking for a fresh start after leaving a role, job, or field due to burnout and hoping to avoid a repeat performance.

Healing is going to look different for different people. Depending on your context, *managing* symptoms related to burnout may be your goal, even if you wish that it could really be fully *healing* from burnout with the time and space for complete *recovery*. If your goal is managing burnout, because you're in a context where you're called to endure despite the stress, because of financial reasons and/or advancement or completing training requirements, here are some internal and external markers that you can use to gauge your success:

- More days than not, you feel recovered (refreshed, replenished) in the morning, or when it's time to return to work or your role or responsibilities.
- You feel engaged throughout most of the day.
- You feel a sense of fulfillment at the end of the day.

- You return to creatively expressing yourself (e.g., writing or creating art or music).
- You rediscover hobbies, interests, and relationships outside of work.
- It feels like there's some distance between you and what stresses you out.
- You feel less cynical and more connected.
- You seek support and community when you begin to feel overwhelmed or alone.

Research shows that some of things that help most with burnout are modifications to the work environment. A few examples include implementing flexible work hours, decreasing workload, increasing paid time off, and enhancing workspace comfort (e.g., addressing noise, temperature, and crowding). It takes power and privilege to have control over your work environment. It's important to recognize that, even if you don't have the power to request or make significant changes, you can still participate in a recovery process and get some relief. Recovery calls for you to disengage, to a certain extent, with whatever is burning you out. If you are a parent, this does *not* mean that you have to get rid of your kids! Research shows that you can build a healthy separation between you and your stress and combat burnout by (1) psychologically detaching sometimes from your role or work, (2) increasing relaxation and a felt sense of peace, and (3) engaging in things away from your stressor that allow you to feel like yourself and like you have a comfortable level of control and influence over yourself and your surroundings.

To help you heal, each of the eight keys offered in this book is designed to

- increase your knowledge about burnout and recovery, as well as your understanding of yourself;

INTRODUCTION xxvii

- give you practical ideas without telling you what you should do;
- simultaneously zoom in to examine fine details and zoom out to consider the bigger picture;
- help you balance your nervous system, so that you can access more of your brain, enhancing your ability to think through complex issues related to work stress and work–life balance;
- support you in envisioning a future with more possibilities that you can look forward to; and
- use the strengths you already have to work toward the changes you hope to see.

SOME ASSURANCES FROM THE AUTHOR

With all the talk in the news and media over the last few years, burnout has become a buzzword, and influencers and advertisers flock to buzzwords, often muddying the waters while trying to market and sell products. It's increasingly easy for words to lose all meaning. As Tricia Hersey (2022), founder of the Nap Ministry and author of *Rest Is Resistance*, notes:

> Another word I wish would be eliminated is *burnout*. It does not get to the heart of the issue. This culture prefers to give things shallow names in an effort to minimize. What if we started to say this when speaking about our career/work life stress: "Trauma is showing up in my body and soul because this culture overworks us like machines."

I've used the word *burnout* for this book title and throughout mainly because it's the search term readers who need this resource will most likely use. But because the term has become so loaded, and because there's so much pseudoscience and marketing jargon orbiting it on social media, I want to offer some assurances as you are beginning to read.

First, you won't be told to "just get some rest," have "better boundaries," or sign up for yoga. I cannot possibly know what you need better than you do—*you* are the expert on yourself. But I have loads of ideas and tips to offer, because I've served so many clients struggling through burnout, and personally had to learn to find my own way back to myself. You'll enjoy and prefer certain keys and activities more than others, and that's okay, and fully expected, because I'm trying to include a wide range of ideas for a wide range of readers.

Second, you won't feel schooled on the same tired stress management techniques you've heard a million times before. Instead, I hope you come away with a more nuanced understanding of your body, brain, and nervous system. I am also honest with you when certain techniques or activities might require more rest and less stress than you're currently able to manage, and I invite you to try alternatives.

Third, a solid examination of burnout calls for *intersectionality*. In "Demarginalizing the Intersection of Race and Sex," American critical race scholar, Kimberlé Crenshaw, says, "Intersectionality is a metaphor for understanding the ways that multiple forms of inequality or disadvantage sometimes compound themselves and create obstacles that often are not understood among conventional ways of thinking" (1989, p. 139). Intersectionality shows you how to appreciate the way sexism *and* racism can impact one person in simultaneous, intersecting ways. Even if they're in the same workplace, a nurse who is a straight white woman with generational wealth will have a different burnout experience than a nurse who is a queer Black woman from a working class family, for instance. I address context—our country's roots in capitalism, white supremacy (which includes patriarchy, misogyny, and ableism), and settler colonialism—and how the game is rigged against all of us, especially those who have historically been targets of marginalization, systemic oppression, exploitation, and violence. You will not be made to feel blamed for your burnout; instead, the cure for burnout is defined here as "not just more self-care . . . [but] all of us caring for each other" (Nagoski & Nagoski, 2019). I hope to help you feel empowered to do something to relieve your symptoms, even in an unjust society.

Fourth, if any of my language has you thinking, *Mercy, she's going to try to cram a bunch of politics down my throat*, you can rest easy—or at least read on before you decide. Teaching, writing, and being a counselor involve very personal work, and the personal is political. I deeply admire and love the clients and students I serve who are liberal and progressive. And I deeply admire and love the clients and students I serve who are conservative. My aim is to show you some doorways into new ways of thinking, not to try to push you through. If you are here only to learn some cutting-edge ways to work with your neurobiology, you can easily pick and choose those bits.

Fifth, you will notice I actively work to center readers who have less power and privilege than I do as a white, upper-middle-class, able-bodied woman. Just because I appreciate how our identities impact us doesn't mean I think, for a common example, that someone hasn't struggled or suffered if they also have economic or white privilege. This is not a competition where we try to compare and rank who has the worst case of burnout—it's about speaking up and being real about the uneven playing field.

Sixth, I'm an evidence-chasing researcher *and* a deeply spiritual person. I don't practice a particular religion, but I feel deeply connected to our human family and think therapists who don't ask about religion and spirituality miss a lot of opportunities. Research shows that if you *do* practice a religion or have your own way of embodying spirituality—even just cultivating wonder and awe—this can be an incredible source of strength when it comes to healing and emotional wellness. That said, I don't have an agenda. I want to respectfully honor and make room for what you hold closest to your heart.

Seventh, if you are a caregiver, in any caregiving role, whose labor receives no financial compensation (e.g., stay-at-home parent, or caring for parents), research shows that you burn out at rates similar to emergency room doctors. Trust that, as you read through this book, your emotional, intellectual, and physical labor will not be written off, and your emotional experiences won't be downplayed or invalidated.

Last but not least, there is no one-size-fits-all approach to mental health or healing through burnout. It's a very personal thing. If you're not in talk therapy and presently feel no wish to even think about it, I'm not going to tell you that you have to go to therapy. Some people heal in community with people who share similar spiritual beliefs. Others do best connecting with themselves and their ancestors through traditional healers and practices that align with their culture more than Western psychotherapy. If you've never talked to any professional ever, you will hear me invite you to engage your curiosity around experimenting with it, particularly if you persistently find yourself hitting a wall and unable to find your way out of the darkness.

DISCLAIMERS

Clinically it can be tricky sometimes to tell the difference between depression and anxiety and burnout. This book provides some self-diagnostic tools but is not intended for assessment and diagnostic purposes. A psychiatrist or psychologist can assist in determining an official diagnosis. Mistaking major depression plus burnout for just burnout, for instance, can leave you working harder than you need to, just to feel okay. In such cases, even if you would not consider medication on a long-term basis, you could use it just for a period if you start feeling your life is too difficult to manage. Even the best swimmers sometimes wear life-preservers when they're navigating risky conditions. And if you're already taking medication(s) but continuing to feel worse, it can be useful to reevaluate with your doctor if it's been a while.

Second, as you're reading or trying some of the activities, if you notice a significant increase in trauma symptoms, distress, or loss of emotional balance (e.g., panic attacks, flashbacks, insomnia or sleep disturbances like night terrors, suicidal ideation, or return of

INTRODUCTION xxxi

symptoms that haven't showed up for a while, such as OCD or disordered eating), please stop reading immediately and consult with a psychotherapist or psychiatrist before continuing.

Third, if you have any underlying conditions that haven't been diagnosed or aren't being treated, you could make all the changes and try all the things suggested here but notice it feels like you keep hitting a wall. It could be worth stopping in for an assessment with a therapist to rule out conditions that may need a higher level of care before burnout symptoms ease up, such as complex PTSD, major depression, anxiety, ADHD, OCD, and/or autism. Once I started understanding and treating my ADHD, for example, a lot of the low feelings and blue mood I had misattributed to burnout shifted.

Fourth, even if you're not into hiring a therapist right now, I highly recommend recruiting a trusted confidant you can confide in about your burnout experience. Especially if you're in stressful fields like medicine, government, or armed services, the culture around addressing mental health can range from secretive to downright hostile—I get the need for privacy! But the more dangerous things will fester and grow in the darkness of isolation and secrecy. I'll tell you more about the Harvard Adult Development Study later, but one thing it shows is that having even just one person who has your back when needed will make you live longer and lower your risk of heart attack, stroke, and dementia.

And lastly, sometimes, to be frank, you're burnt out mostly because you're surrounded by selfish people taking advantage of you with zero motivation to stop, because they are financially, intellectually, and/or emotionally benefitting from your labor. If you go to therapy when needed, take pretty good care of yourself most of the time, and try every suggestion in this book, and your symptoms don't ease up *at all*—it might be your sign to step back and discern if you possibly need to change environments. It can be heartbreaking to make a decision to walk away from something you feel could be a great fit *if only*: If only the owner and his son could grow up and learn to actually listen to their employees, if only the manager could get their anger managed during stressful shifts. . . . This book offers resources to help you think through tough decisions like whether or not to stay at a workplace or in a career or role where you're burning out.

SOME EMERGENCY RESOURCES

Mental health professionals have been trained for decades to recommend first calling 911 in the case of a life-threatening emergency. However, it's critical to recognize and acknowledge that, depending on where you live and what you look like, involving local police may *not* actually be the safest thing to do in *every* mental health crisis. Additionally, I recommend you search "24-hour crisis line" in your area and save that number to your phone—this is a smart, harm-reduction step for just about anyone. Local resources like this are great for when you're thinking, *I don't know what to do, but I don't think I can keep myself safe right now*, or *I don't know how to proceed—someone I love is experiencing a mental health crisis and is putting themselves or others in danger*.

Here are some national resources that can also be helpful, regardless of where you are in the United States:

24-Hour Suicide and Crisis Lifeline (English/Spanish):
Call/Text 988

Crisis Text Line:
Text "HOME" to 741741

National Domestic Violence Hotline:
1-(800)-799-7233

LGBT Trevor Project Lifeline:
1-(866)-488-7386

National Sexual Assault Hotline:
1-(800)-656-4673

Department of Labor, to file a complaint:
1-(866)-487-9243

National Domestic Workers Alliance:
646-360-5806

Resources, fact sheets, quick links, and information on U.S. worker rights:
https://www.dol.gov/agencies/whd/workers

8 KEYS TO HEALING, MANAGING, AND PREVENTING BURNOUT

KEY 1

Identify and Appreciate Your Own Social, Cultural, and Psychological Risks

> You're burned out because this culture has messed up our priorities, not because there's something wrong with you.
>
> —JULIANA FINCH

> [Burnout] isn't a personal problem. It's a societal one—and it will not be cured by productivity apps, or a bullet journal, or face mask skin treatments, or overnight fucking oats.
>
> —ANNE HELEN PETERSEN

It's silly to try to assess and treat burnout without taking a look at the *whole* picture of what someone is going through. As a clinician, I ask about health and wellness, sometimes recommending bloodwork and sleep studies. I collaborate with psychiatrists and consider their assessments. We compassionately address substance use issues. Clients and I take a look at relationships—with lovers, partners, friends, family, loved ones, and key players like coworkers and mentors. I'll sometimes refer an individual client to couple therapy with their partner. We discuss marital and parental status, history with grief and loss, if any. We discuss culture, parents, and grandparents, and track multigenerational family patterns. I take a deep look at emotions, cognitions, and behaviors. We think through early life—beliefs gained and memories held in their body. I check for trauma. I ask about existential things—the heavy philosophical stuff that has to do with existence, being human, and what gives you meaning and purpose—and about religion and spirituality. I assess safety and check for possible risks. I also invite clients to share about things like race, gender, sexuality, and ability status. We talk about socioeconomic status and power and privilege, especially in the context of work life. Humans are too social, too multifaceted to examine without considering the *entire* context in which they work and live.

So, I'll invite you to approach yourself with a similar, holistic approach. I'm going to introduce a topic now that sometimes gets met with eye rolls these days, especially when I'm speaking down here in Texas. If you are someone who feels easily annoyed with topics like social justice, I'm going to ask you to roll with me here for a couple of pages—especially if you've never really thought or read much about how things like the impact of race and gender on burnout. As I've mentioned, I love the clients I serve—the progressive ones, the leftists, the conservative ones, and everyone in between. I'm also keenly aware that I'm writing during an unprecedented time with respect to politics and technology in the United States and globally. There's a lot of polarization and animosity right now. I want to be incredibly clear here that I'm not trying to push a politic. *And*, you'll be missing a big part of the picture if we don't kick off from a foundation that includes such things as power, privilege, and justice. If this is old news for you, thanks for letting me preach to the choir, and if you're going out on a limb with me here, thanks for your openness.

Where I'm from in the South, there can be this sentiment that talking about these sorts of things—equity, justice, the history of oppression—amounts to just drudging up the past, old news, just to make us feel bad about ourselves: "borrowing trouble," "beating a dead horse." This is absolutely *not* what I'm up to here. This isn't an invitation for white or privileged people to self-flagellate, shame spiral, or play whose burnout is the worst. I only wish to highlight how wise it is to appreciate how your social and cultural contexts impact your story, which impacts your experience of burnout. Healing calls for each of us to recognize just how much of what we struggle against comes from things intentionally woven into the fabric of our lives as citizens. So my only ask is that you check out the next few paragraphs. You will probably enjoy most of the activities in this book regardless of how you think about the world!

When discussing power and privilege, you may hear these things defined in terms of what some people *have*, such as special access, that others do not have. Often, though, privilege involves what one does *not have* to do, such as avoiding obstacles that others must trudge through. I recently wanted to have some routine testing done, so I made an appointment, but when I showed up the clinic informed me my insurance would cover the costs only if I first went to a primary care doctor to get a referral. Because I was about to travel and couldn't take off any more time from work, *and* because I can afford a random, out-of-pocket expense, I got to see the doctor that day—I didn't have to wait, and I didn't have to disrupt my life or clients' and students' lives by having to reschedule and jump through more hoops before receiving the care I needed.

This example might sound simple, but when it comes to burnout, "simple" things become big things, and as they pile up—it's death by a thousand cuts. And sometimes it's more clear-cut. Women in my state have been bleeding out in parking lots, waiting until they are close enough to death, before they can be helped, because of state legislation. And it only takes a quick peek at the research on health outcomes for Americans of color to know that stressors, from work to forces like racism and sexism, have a literal, physical impact on health and well-being. The Centers for Disease Control and Prevention reports that Black women are almost *three times* more likely than white women to die giving birth (Centers for Disease Control and Prevention, 2024). The disparities extend to all sorts of health conditions, from cardiovascular issues to diabetes. To not recognize the ways that social and political systems literally, physically impact our bodies and our lives is to miss a profoundly critical piece of the burnout puzzle. A few quick examples: If you have a diagnosis like autism, sensory processing disorder, or ADHD, you may also have a greater risk for burnout. And certain conditions, if nothing else, make burnout feel so much more miserable and unmanageable—looking at you, people with multiple sclerosis, chronic fatigue syndrome, rheumatoid arthritis, psoriasis, chronic pain conditions, long COVID, chronic migraines, chronic bowel disease like Crohn's, and/or endometriosis, to name just a few.

If you're a working parent and/or caregiver, you are especially set up for experiencing burnout. When I say *caregiver*, this includes caring for a disabled or sick partner, child, family member, or loved one. Have you heard the phrase *sandwich generation*? It refers to caring for both children and aging parents, at the same time. Boomers and, increasingly, Gen X and millennials know how draining this experience can be. It can feel lonely while at the same time you are desperate for alone time. I have so many friends and clients who work as nurses while also being/becoming parents that I really get a front-row seat for some of the challenges. I repeatedly hear that parenting is harder than work, if for no other reason than the never-ending nature of it. At work, you can clock out and trust your colleagues to hold things steady until you return. You eventually forget the name of the patient who called you slurs. Even if it feels like you don't get to very often, it *is* possible to step away. But as a parent, even if you are incredibly supported with childcare and help, things like mom guilt or simply longing for precious time with your little ones can make it tough to even *want* to step away—even if you know that you need some solitude and connection with adults to feel more yourself. And the same goes for many caregivers! Especially if you know that you have a limited amount of time left with someone, it can feel incredibly challenging to make time for yourself. It can be too easy to tell yourself the story that it's selfish or wrong, somehow, to not be there, helping all the time.

I want to invite you to think about these stressors as *layers*. Imagine someone who grew up in poverty and has PTSD from being abused by their family and more PTSD from continuing abuse from romantic partners and is disabled from being a victim of a mass shooting. Imagine a parent who has a degenerative spinal disease and is diagnosed with depression and is getting laid off. Imagine someone else who is autistic and is a Black man and is homeless. Imagine another who is Latino and has asthma and is undocumented and has PTSD from escaping a dangerous environment with his family. This isn't to say that the more layers you have, the weaker you are. When I think about who burns out most severely among people I have served, it's usually clients with the most layers who also learned to try to "tough it out" and "grin and bear it," even when things are difficult and painful, even when they are isolated and trying to do everything on their own. Sometimes I end up being one of the only people who knows just how heavy and hopeless they feel. They will say there's just no other choice but to power through—"I'll sleep when I'm dead!" Parents and caregivers frequently say the same. So, there are concrete reasons that the most marginalized and minoritized end up with higher rates of cardiovascular disease, diabetes, and cancer.

Just so we're crystal clear, I'm not saying that, in order to combat burnout effectively, you must become anticapitalist. But, you need to be able to see and acknowledge that, in a nation with a history of white settler colonialism and chattel slavery, capitalism impacts the lives of citizens, for both good *and* bad! You can be a serious capitalist and still appreciate that much of the colonized world was built on ground stolen from Indigenous people, and quite literally on the backs of enslaved people. Ironically, when slavery was abolished in the United States, many slavers were even compensated financially with reparations for the loss of their livelihood. (If this doesn't sound familiar, search "compensated emancipation" online.) Any analysis of burnout and exploitation of Americans is simply incomplete if it fails to zoom out far enough historically and socioculturally. We didn't just trip and slip into being a nation that "pulls itself up by its bootstraps!"

So, if you're a person who has a lot of power and privilege, you're not being called to explore this as some exercise in self-punishment or shame. Rather, being aware of how both privilege and stressors affect you and those around you will empower you to better advocate, address, and avoid burnout. If you *do not* have lots of power and privilege, it's critical to appreciate the ways this compounds the weight of burnout. If you *do* have more privilege, it's essential to appreciate all the things you have access to, and the many hurdles you get to avoid, so that you can more effectively leverage your power and help advocate for change, both in your own life and in the lives of others.

THEORY AND BACKGROUND

The more resources and power you have, the more protected you are from exploitation and oppression. In many cases it's safe to swap the term *burnt out* for *exploited*. For the record, just because you aren't working at a paying job outside your home doesn't mean no one will exploit you. (All you default parents reading this, who are responsible for most of the care tasks, are nodding your heads.) When you are treated as less than human, like a machine, it can be eerily easy to fall into a habit of not "humaning," as many clients say—you lose touch with what's natural. You stop doing the things bodies need to do to release and move through stress, or you do them in ways that transform pleasure into more work, such as forcing excessive, strenuous exercise to fit some social standard, rather than including joyful movement in your life to stay strong and healthy and keep your mind sharp.

Therapist Cloé Madanes outlined six core human needs that I share with clients when discussing burnout. We tend to feel most whole and human—not burnt out—when these needs are consistently attended to:

- Certainty
- Variety
- Significance
- Connection
- Growth
- Contribution

What do you notice about your internal reaction to reading these core needs? When I share this list with people who are really burnt out, their response is usually a combination of a scoff, a laugh, and an eye roll, along with a sardonic "Wouldn't *that* be nice!" When you feel so exhausted, it feels like a challenge even to keep yourself fed and clean; things like connection, growth, significance, and contribution can seem like pie in the sky. But the more you intentionally carve out space—little bits here and there—to honor these six very basic, very human needs, the more protected you will be from burning out. We will think through these in more depth coming up.

Please note: Perfectionism is an incredibly common trait/tendency among those I serve who tend to burn out. Because of this, I want to be clear that, when I share a list like this, it is not an invitation to make sure every single day includes equal proportions of each of these six things. A healthy goal sounds more like, "More weeks than not, throughout the year, I'm making sure to get a good amount of each of these six things," or "More of these needs than not are being met to a decent extent a majority of the time."

When you think about the fabric of your day-to-day life, in the current season, which of these core needs do you feel like you're already meeting well or pretty well? If you're like, "Um—none?" allow me to offer an obnoxious consolation prize: that's really normal for people feeling burnt out. You may be thinking, "Well, I'm *certain* that I'm not getting variety or significance or growth or much connection. So, I guess there's certainty!"

When you think back on your childhood, how consistently were these six needs met? Your answer may very well be related to what I introduced earlier in this chapter: Experiences like poverty, racism, sexism, ableism, body shaming, immigration, and/or misogyny, and many more, impact our experiences with these six core needs. If your parents struggled to keep the utilities running, certainty was probably not on the menu very often. You may have experienced a similar level of uncertainty if you grew up in a military family and were frequently moved from place to place. Therapy clients with these experiences often share some version of, "The only thing you could predict was that things would be unpredictable." Variety, on the other hand, may have been abundant. In contrast, variety may have also been in short supply if you grew up poor, or if your family had plenty of money but subscribed to restrictive religious practices. If you grew up on a dirt road out in the middle of nowhere, you might have had to get creative by connecting with animals, such as cats, dogs, and horses, especially if you didn't feel safe or accepted in your family. So, although it is true that access to wealth makes meeting many of these needs a lot more feasible, on the flipside, some of the wealthiest people I've served have been the most profoundly unhappy.

Social support and connection are two other extremely protective factors with respect to how burnout shows up (or doesn't), regardless of sociocultural factors. Tons of studies show that social support—people in our lives we trust to have our back—can lessen the negative effects of stress on health and even help prevent burnout (Hold-Lunsta et al., 2010; Hou et al., 2020; Mikkola et al., 2018; Ruisoto et al., 2021). And this doesn't mean that you suddenly need to become extroverted, if you're not a very social person. One of the longest ongoing studies of adult life, the Harvard Study of Adult Development (begun in 1938 and carried out by multiple generations of researchers), has shown that having even just one person in your corner who you feel has your back through the ups and downs in life, you'll

- live longer,
- be less likely to experience cardiovascular events like heart attack and stroke, and
- be less likely to develop dementias and will have later onset if you eventually do.

One of the big social risk factors for burning out is isolation, even a felt sense of isolation while there are people around you. It's no surprise, when you know the science. But I promise you, I won't tell you just to go and make a bunch of new friends, like that's *the* solution to your burnout. Especially since the pandemic, I've seen so many clients, especially those who are immunocompromised, sick, and/or disabled, connecting online in incredibly meaningful ways with friends they often never would have met in person. Connection can take all kinds of forms. I hope that, if you don't already, you'll come to appreciate (a) the extent to which human bodies evolved a need for connection and (b) the measurable, negative impacts of loneliness and the felt sense of aloneness—especially during times of stress and crisis. Do you live and work far away from your family or chosen family? Do you have friends at work? How about friends outside of work or, if you work at home, outside the home? Do you get to have enjoyable, grown-up conversations with adults too, no matter how much you adore your kids?

One final bit of theory is about early life and how it impacts health and wellness later in life. In 1998, the Centers for Disease Control partnered with Kaiser Permanente to study the links between adult health risk behaviors and childhood abuse and household dysfunction. The study is known as The Adverse Childhood Experiences (ACE) study and was published in the *American Journal of Preventative Medicine* (Felitti et al., 1998). Findings from the initial study and follow up (ACE Response, n.d.) found that people who experienced four or more adverse childhood events had (para. 6):

- Increased risk for smoking, alcoholism, and drug abuse
- Increased risk for depression and suicide attempts
- Poor self-rated health
- Greater likelihood of sexually transmitted disease
- Challenges with physical inactivity, and severe obesity
- Likelihood of attempted suicide across the lifespan
- Increased risk for broken bones
- Heart disease
- Lung disease
- Liver disease
- Multiple types of cancer

You will see a complete list of the adverse experiences from the original and expanded studies in an upcoming activity, but some brief examples: witnessing domestic violence, experiencing abuse or neglect, caregivers' mental health challenges (e.g., substance use issues, suicide), experiencing racism or bullying, and being in foster care (Felitti et al., 1998; Cronholm et al., 2015). Research from the CDC shows that as the number of ACEs increases, so does the risk for negative health outcomes (Centers for Disease Control and Prevention, 2021). The CDC (2021) also lists the following statistics:

- 1 in 6 adults experienced four or more types of ACEs
- At least 5 of the top 10 leading causes of death are associated with ACEs
- Preventing ACEs could reduce the number of adults with depression by as much as 44% (BRFSS 2015–2017, 25 states, CDC Vital Signs, November 2019)

> As social critic and poet bell hooks has noted, "The first act of violence that patriarchy demands of males is not violence toward women. Instead patriarchy demands of all males that they engage in psychic self-mutilation, that they kill off the emotional parts of themselves. If an individual is not successful in emotionally crippling himself, he can count on patriarchal men to enact rituals of power that will assault his self-esteem" (hooks, 2004).

As a therapist I've noticed that ACEs are associated with increased rates of burnout among clients. And research backs me up. One study on physicians found that those with four or more ACEs scored 2.5 times higher on burnout measures than those without ACEs (Yellowlees et al., 2021). In research on nursing students, Gloria McKee-Lopez and her colleagues (2019) found that "the number of reported ACEs by participants had a significant relationship on the levels of burnout and severity of depressive symptom," and noted further that female students with a higher number of ACEs were more likely to report higher levels of burnout, and higher depression severity than their male counterparts (Abstract). What's important for you to appreciate here is that having a bunch of ACEs doesn't mean you're not strong or resilient, but it *does* mean you're more likely to experience burnout. And further, aspects of your identity like race and gender—back to that concept of intersectionality—will also layer in to impact burnout intensity.

DISCOVERING THE KEY

After almost a decade of serving clients as a therapist, it's incredibly clear to me that burnout is more manageable when you make sure to address two critical pieces: (a) sociocultural and political factors and (b) emotional attunement and interpersonal relationships. Because so much of the injury of burnout has to do with aloneness, it makes sense that so many of the containers for healing look relational. But because we live in a society that values individualism so highly, many of the typical approaches to helping someone who is burnt out are overly individualistic. This is not to say that, if you don't currently have community or close connections, you're doomed to be burnt out forever—far from it. *And*, I continually observe clients feeling less stuck when they begin to focus more on connecting with others, as well as strengthening and improving those relationships. The thought, "I'm totally alone in this," is like rot. As social creatures wired to connect and depend on others, our bodies experience more of the toxic effects of stress when in isolation or perceived isolation. To be clear, you can prefer to be alone in solitude most of the time and still thrive—it's more about the *felt*-sense of aloneness, or loneliness. And the antidote is the opposite: it's about the felt-sense of connection, a sense of belonging.

As little ones, survival quite literally depended on others. As you read in the theory and background section, human bodies, brains, and minds work best when you don't feel alone. Long story short: you become what you need to be accepted and protected. Then as you grow and gain more independence, you keep all of the parts of yourself that were born to make sense of and survive that early environment, but you also evolve and develop other parts of yourself. I grew up in a house with a "no whining" policy. There's a part of me that seeks to avoid self-pity, sometimes in extreme or unhelpful ways. This sometimes makes it hard for me even to ask for help, share when I'm struggling, or receive someone's condolences. I share this because I know I'm not the only one who grew up with this, and it's important to recognize unhealthy messages you received growing up so that you can allow yourself to acknowledge, validate, and accept your struggles in the healthy ways necessary to address burnout. Research continues to show that practicing what's called *self-compassion*—turning compassion inward, being warm and understanding toward yourself when you feel inadequate, fail, or suffer, as opposed to ignoring the pain or being self-critical—helps reduce anxiety symptoms and improve mental and emotional well-being. You will learn a lot more about concrete ways to incorporate self-compassion into your life later in this book.

I share all of this because clients often reflect how relieving it can feel just to have a word for something previously unnamed. A classic therapist saying is, "What's mentionable is manageable." Dan Siegel, founder of the field of interpersonal neurobiology, says "name it to tame it." Even if you can't resolve or fix something, just having it acknowledged can feel so good—putting words to your internal experiences calms your body. From a *very* general perspective on neuroscience, your amygdala—the little part in your brain that focuses on threat detection—loves it when you use words to describe sensations, feelings, and experiences in general. Humans are connecting creatures, and create reality, together by sharing language, and learn by watching and imitating. The stories you tell to yourself and to others are incredibly relevant to your mental health and well-being—and to the wellness of those you love. A lot of peace and healing can come from selecting a trustworthy listener to be with you and be a witness as you say what's true to and for you.

This can get complex fast. I work in the middle of a very emotion-dismissing region where many of us are raised being told (with and without words) that having feelings is weak and problematic and that there's no point in "wallowing" or "bellyaching." Even now as an adult, when I trip and fall, without fail the first voice I hear is, "You're fine! Get up and brush it off!" Men and masculine people get an extra heavy dose of this emotion-avoiding training. Women and femmes might get written off as being hysterical for feeling and sharing about emotion, but at least they're socially more permitted to *express*. Regarding emotional expression, more than a few men I've worked with here in Texas have told me their fathers just instructed them to "drink it down with brown," that is, try to use booze to push emotions too far down to be felt. (Those of you who have seen loved ones with black eyes or holes punched into drywall know how poorly this usually goes.) I just want to normalize that, depending on how you were brought up in the world, your knee-jerk reaction might be to feel that talking about emotions, culture, or our social condition is pointless, or even overly self-centered. I am here to tell you that you deserve the wellness and freedom that come with healthy emotional expression. It may take some practice and getting used to, but it's absolutely possible for you to grow.

ACTIVITIES

These four activities are opportunities to experiment with the ideas we've discussed surrounding this first key. For example, how helpful *is* it to acknowledge and appreciate factors beyond your control impacting your day-to-day life? Is it a little easier not to blame yourself or consider yourself a failure for burning out when you take time to zoom out and appreciate your context within a very complex system? Does a part of you feel like you are "making excuses" when you acknowledge the factors that make you more likely or less likely to suffer through burnout than other people with different sociocultural backgrounds and conditions?

ACTIVITY 1A
BURNOUT RISK-FACTOR CHECKLIST

Goal
To recognize if you are in an environment, a life stage, or a role making it likely that you can experience burnout, and consider what changes, or requests for changes, you could make (given your amount of power, authority, or voice in the system) to reduce or minimize risk for burnout.

Instructions
First, please look through the checklists below. Then, complete the checklist that fits your situation: the *employment checklist* if you are employed, or the *caregiver checklist* if you are a caregiver not currently working outside that role. Place a check mark beside each item that feels true for you right now. Then, complete the prompt that comes after your checklist. If you are a parent, you can also use the checklist at the end of this activity for a bit more guidance in self-assessing whether or not you may be experiencing parenting burnout specifically.

Stress and Burnout Risk-Factor Checklist: Employment

- ❏ I have a heavy workload and work long hours.
- ❏ I struggle with work–life balance—work takes up so much time and energy it feels like there's nothing left for family and friends.
- ❏ I work in a helping profession, such as health care or childcare.
- ❏ My work involves a high level of legal liability.
- ❏ I feel I have little or no control over my work or schedule.
- ❏ What I do was not my first choice of career.

❑ My work does not provide clear expectations—I feel unclear about my authority and what others expect from me.
❑ In terms of activity, my work involves extremes of monotony and/or chaos.
❑ My work is unpredictable.
❑ The values of my work organization, institution, or boss don't match up well with my personal values.
❑ Understaffing is an issue where I work.
❑ The effort I put in feels greater than the reward or compensation I receive.
❑ I don't receive as much recognition and gratitude as I would like for my work.
❑ There are dysfunctional dynamics in my workplace (e.g., bully, unfair supervisor, micromanaging boss).
❑ I feel isolated.
❑ I don't have strong social support networks.
❑ I don't have a supportive partner(s).
❑ I regularly get less than 7 hours of sleep per night.
❑ I'm not able to get more sleep than usual on weekends to recover.
❑ Finances are a struggle.
❑ I have one or more of the following tendencies: perfectionism, people-pleasing, self-sacrificing, overachieving, high empathy.
❑ I don't have any hobbies or sources of entertainment and pleasure outside of work.

The more items you checked as *true*, the greater your risk for experiencing burnout, according to research (Adriaenssens et al., 2015; Bährer-Kohler, 2013; Jovanović et al., 2016; Talavera-Velasco et al., 2018; Trockel et al., 2023).

Stress and Burnout Risk-Factor Checklist: Caregiving

- ❏ There's no way to make the care receiver "well."
- ❏ An extreme degree of physical and emotional care is needed.
- ❏ My workload feels overwhelming.
- ❏ I have conflicting demands (i.e., the care receiver's needs conflict with the needs of my children, spouses, employers, etc.).
- ❏ I have no time to be alone or really get much privacy at all.
- ❏ I have no choice about being a caregiver.
- ❏ I care for someone who needs constant care.
- ❏ I care for a spouse.
- ❏ I face money problems.
- ❏ I live with the person who needs care.
- ❏ I feel alone, helpless, or depressed.
- ❏ I don't have good coping or problem-solving skills.
- ❏ I feel the need to give care at all times.
- ❏ I feel like I get little guidance from health care professionals.

The more items you checked as *true*, the greater your risk is for experiencing caregiver stress and burnout, according to research (Mayo Clinic Staff, 2023; Johns Hopkins Bayview, n.d.).

Please note: I don't share this list so that you can do the opposite of each item as some solution. It's important to recognize how many interacting factors are at play here. If you fail to appreciate how dynamic burnout is, it can be easy to blame yourself. And the very last thing you need when you are already feeling squished under the weight of burnout is the added burdens of blame and shame. My hope is that the direction you go with it will sound more like, "Whoa—of course I'm burnt out! This isn't some personal failing or character flaw. I'm not broken."

Journaling Prompts

When you see a recommendation to journal, first I'd like to invite you to find a place that is as free from interruption as possible. If you're able, I find that most clients get more from writing by hand as opposed to typing, but you may certainly type or take notes on your phone if you know that works better for you. Depending on you and your story, a prompt could take anywhere from a few minutes to an hour or so to contemplate and write about. Since there will be so many opportunities to journal in this book, I recommend getting a notepad or notebook specifically for this purpose to keep with your book as you read. You know you better than I do, so I trust you to discern how much is helpful for you to write down! A few notes in the margins might be perfectly fine for you.

> What's is like for you to look at your list? I'm sure you're not sitting there shocked and awed, but what thoughts and feelings pop up? If it feels right for you, take a few moments to journal about this. I want to acknowledge that it's normal to feel an increase in hopelessness as you begin to look at your burnout, especially if it's not something you've really examined before or very deeply.

> How does it feel thinking about these risk factors and your experiences? Take a moment to journal. If you have any feelings of guilt or sadness coming up, please feel invited to make room for that in whatever way feels comfortable.

> When you think about your story and the individual factors and experiences that shape and impact you, aside from what you've seen on these research-based checklists, is there anything else you think sets you up for burning out?

> Do you think your marginalized or minoritized identities (e.g., being LGBTQIA+, disabled, a woman, a Black American, low-income, etc.) impact these risk factors in an intersectional way? How? (For example, *If I wasn't* _____ , *I don't think I'd be experiencing* ___.)

IDENTIFY AND APPRECIATE YOUR OWN RISKS

Please note: Parents, if you are not sure if you are experiencing parenting burnout, depression, or parenting stress, Roskam et al. (2018) developed the Parental Burnout Assessment, which found four factors to consider:

- ❏ Exhaustion related to your parental role
- ❏ Emotional distance from your kids
- ❏ Feelings of being fed up with your parental role
- ❏ Contrast with how you used to be and how you want to be

How does parenting impact your experience of burnout? Do you actually love work outside the home but feel burnt out mainly from responsibilities with kids, spouse, and home? Or vice versa: Do you hate work but feel recharged by your parenting role? Or, are you struggling with *both*?

Relational Activity Add-On: Ask your partner, friend, loved one, or mentor to complete the same checklist(s). Are they also at risk for burning out? You probably won't be surprised if they are.

ACTIVITY 1B
The Story of Grind Culture in My Family

> Grind culture is a collaboration between white supremacy and capitalism. It views our divine bodies as machines. Our worth is not connected to how much we produce. Another way is possible.
>
> —TRICIA HERSEY

Goal
To explore the culture and values in your family and community that turn into beliefs and values that can increase your risk for burnout.

Instructions

Below is a list of questions for you to read through to prompt journaling, thinking, or even discussion with a trusted loved one. If your relationship can support the vulnerability, it can also be illuminating and validating for adult children to ask the person or people who raised you questions like these too.

> How did/do your caregiver(s) or family define *success*? How do you know this? (For example, "They told me flat out," or "They told stories about family members they were proud of and compared/contrasted them to me," or "They acted disappointed and treated me poorly if x/y/z.")
>
> How does your family's culture and/or history play into your values around work? (For example, "My parents are immigrants to the United States with a strong work ethic so I would not even let them catch me sitting still or relaxing growing up because I'd get scolded," or "I'm a third-generation firefighter, and our values are overtly named as part of our legacy," or "I grew up in poverty with a single parent—not working was never an option and I never leave a gig unless there's already new one lined up for sure.")
>
> What did you learn about self-sacrifice growing up? How? What do you currently believe? How do you feel about the saying, "Don't light yourself on fire to keep others warm"?
>
> Did anyone you looked up to growing up use phrases like *hustle* or *grind*? "Sleep when you're dead"? "No rest for the weary"? Anything similar? Were you encouraged to have multiple side hustles?
>
> Was working hard glorified—even if it hurt you or caused health problems? Did anyone around you seem proud of how they struggled? How did they show that? Did you get the message that success requires extreme struggle and suffering? Or that you would grow up right only if you struggled as much as your parent(s)?

Did your family talk differently about work or about values based on gender? If expectations of "hard work" were different based on gender, what did you learn?

How would your family define *hard work*? How about *laziness*? What stories were told about family members or others to exemplify either hard work or laziness? Do you see your family's cultural background playing into these definitions and values? How?

What does "good enough" mean in your family or community? Does it feel like they have overly high standards and you could never really satisfy them? Or does it feel like the bar is very low and no one really cares? How did you get this message?

Did you see caregivers or anyone in your family model rest? Did you see anyone take naps or schedule leisure time? Was there a sense that you could rest or have fun only as a reward for working hard enough?

Outside of workplace hustle-and-grind values, what messages did you receive about duty at home, in the family? What was expected from the caregivers in your family? Was "suffering in silence" celebrated or glorified? Is there a memory or story that exemplifies this?

Did your religious or spiritual upbringing impact messages you received about hard work or suffering without complaining? What's that like to think about now?

ACTIVITY 1C
Adverse Childhood Experience Questionnaire for Adults

> Shouting self-care at people who actually need community care is how we fail them.
>
> —NIKITA VALERIO

Goal

To briefly/rapidly recognize trauma and adverse childhood experiences and appreciate that how our nervous system gets wired colors burnout symptoms and behavioral responses to stressors.

Instructions

First, please be sure that you are in a safe, private space where you feel comfortable. You are going to be asked about some possibly painful memories and experiences. If you get flooded or overwhelmed by emotion, please feel invited to stop the activity and take care of yourself before continuing.

Below is a list of 10 categories of adverse childhood experiences (ACEs) from the original study. Then, there is another list from the Philadelphia ACE Survey, which expanded the original list to include more things at the community level (https://www.philadelphiaaces.org/philadelphia-ace-survey). Please place a checkmark next to each category that you experienced prior to your 18th birthday. Then, please add up the number of categories of ACEs you experience and put the total number at the bottom. If you feel up for it, go through the journaling prompts afterward.

Original ACE Checklist
(http://www.aceresponse.org/who_we_are/ACE-Study_43_pg.html)

- ❏ Physical abuse by a parent (e.g., being hit, beaten, kicked)
- ❏ Emotional abuse by a parent (e.g., being sworn at, insult, put down)
- ❏ Sexual abuse by anyone
- ❏ Growing up with an alcohol and/or drug abuser in the household
- ❏ Experiencing the incarceration of a household member
- ❏ Living with a family member experiencing mental illness
- ❏ Domestic violence

IDENTIFY AND APPRECIATE YOUR OWN RISKS

- ❏ Loss of a parent (e.g., divorce, death, abandonment)
- ❏ Emotional neglect (e.g., felt that no one loved you)
- ❏ Physical neglect (e.g., not enough to eat, had to wear dirty clothes)

Expanded ACE Checklist

(https://www.philadelphiaaces.org/philadelphia-ace-survey)

- ❏ Witnessing violence in the community (e.g., stabbings, shootings)
- ❏ Discrimination based on race/ethnicity
- ❏ Adverse neighborhood experiences (not feeling safe in neighborhood)
- ❏ Bullying by peers or classmates
- ❏ Living in foster care

__ **Total ACEs** (number of checked responses)

What was it like to go through this checklist? Had you heard of the ACEs study prior to reading this book? What feelings did you notice as you were reading and responding?

Did you know that higher ACEs scores can be associated with all kinds of health concerns, from heart disease to cancers? Are you currently/recently experiencing any physical symptoms involving pain and/or fatigue? Is there a history of any of these symptoms in your family? (For example, multiple generations in a row on one side have had heart, lung, or liver disease.)

Clients tend to report that going through this ACE checklist feels vulnerable but validating. It brings about a lot of "Oh, *no wonder* I ___," and "*Of course* I have a hard time with ___. I'm not crazy/broken—just human." If this feels tough for you, I will share more information on self-compassion and offer opportunities to practice it throughout the book.

It feels important to say here that it is possible both to be incredibly grateful to those who brought us into the world and raised us and to recognize as adults that some (or most) core needs we had as kids or teens weren't met. You can hold softness and understanding for the fact that caregivers did the best they could do with what they had.

On the flipside, it's also perfectly okay if you feel zero softness and know that what happened wasn't right and there's no forgiving it. I mostly wanted to include the ACE assessment because it's so common for people to downplay life experiences or write them off as not that big of a deal, but science shows that experiencing trauma physically changes our bodies and brains in ways we need to pay attention to.

If you have one or more ACEs and you've never done any therapy, I'd like to acknowledge that so many clients report feeling lighter and more at ease with life when they process those negative experiences and trauma.

> What does processing mean? Processing looks different for everyone, for the record—you may never even need to say your story all the way through out loud, like people often assume therapy requires. If you are thinking you might like to try talking with a trauma-informed therapist, where to begin can feel kind of overwhelming. If you've done therapy before, check out EMDR trauma therapy. If you're brand new to therapy, you might still benefit from EMDR, but I'd invite you to first look into treatments like somatic experiencing therapy, dialectical behavioral therapy, or internal family systems therapy. All of these have solid evidence that they are effective.
>
> And processing also does not have to happen in a Western therapy context. Many people use spiritual or ancestral practices, community experiences, creation (e.g., art, poetry, comedy,

IDENTIFY AND APPRECIATE YOUR OWN RISKS

> music), and a variety of other means to process and safely reprocess traumatic experiences. It will look different based on how you were raised in the world and what your family of origin's culture and emotional tendencies are. One "style" is not universally better than another.

ACTIVITY 1D
Inventory of Toxic Cultural Values

> Change culture and you change lives. You can also change the course of history.
>
> —RESMAA MENAKEM

Goal
To survey some of the characteristics of white supremacist cultures (e.g., the culture in the United States) and take a look at home and work environments, considering how these characteristics dial up the risk for burning out.

Instructions
Below is a list some of the less-than-healthy characteristics and values of white supremacist, patriarchal, and capitalist cultures, taken from Tema Okun and Kenneth Jones's (2001) *Dismantling Racism Workbook*. Please read through the list, and then feel invited to complete the prompts that follow.

- Perfectionism
- Sense of urgency

- Quantity over quality
- "There's only one right way"
- Paternalism
- "Either/or" thinking
- Power hoarding
- Fear of open conflict
- Individualism
- Progress = bigger/more
- Prioritizing comfort of white people

Do you recognize any of your family's or culture's values or characteristics in the list above? Which one(s)? Were they unspoken or explicitly communicated? How about the values at your place of work? Your own personal values?

Which of these characteristic(s) would you say go most with emotional exhaustion for you?

Which people, groups, or systems benefit when you work yourself to death?

When you think about your own experience of burnout, how do you see the items in the list playing into your symptoms (or not)? Is there a colleague or boss who especially embodies something on the list? (For example, "Yes, my supervisor always wants everything perfect—aka, how *they* would do it—and done yesterday.")

Do you have a perfectionist part of yourself? An either/or part? How about a conflict-avoiding part? An inner know-it-all? What happens with these parts of you when you're burning out? How do you see them in your mind's eye? (For example, "My inner perfectionist part has dark circles under her eyes and she's just going in circles straightening and restraightening things, exhausted but unable to sit.")

> Thinking back to Activity 1B, The Story of Grind Culture in My Family, do you think any of the items on the list overlap with characteristics of grind culture? Which ones?

EVALUATE AND PLAN TO USE THIS KEY (OR NOT!)

As each chapter winds down, I want to make sure you have an opportunity to reflect and feel empowered to decide what, if anything, you'd like to take with you from the experience of reading the key and engaging in the activities. Below are some prompts you can use to evaluate and plan.

> How was this first key for you? Any new knowledge or understandings? Any bits or parts you really connected with or liked? Anything you'd like to immediately "return to sender"?
>
> *What I took from this key and the activities was really that* ___ (summarize). (For example, "Burnout isn't a moral or personal failing—it's something bigger than me and doesn't have a simple solution because everyone is different.")
>
> *My specific plan for how I'll use this key is* ___ (e.g., "is to remind myself, when I'm getting self-critical or hard on myself, how many factors are at play and how unfair the system is, and to give myself a little grace that it's not all my fault").

If it feels alright, check in with your body and see if you're needing anything right now. I want to invite you attend to your needs. If there's not time right now, take a look at your calendar and plan a time to circle back and make sure there's nothing in your body asking for your attention. A lot of nurses I've served will say, "If you don't make time to take care of your body, your body will pick a time for you, and it will probably be at a very inconvenient time."

FINAL THOUGHTS

If you don't take an honest look at how the deck is stacked against all of us differently, you run the risk of overly blaming yourself (or others around you!) for perceived personal shortcomings when you're really burning out because you're a human in a system that exploits humans. I'm reminded of the scene in *The Wizard of Oz* when Toto pulls the curtain back and the wizard can be seen saying, "Pay no attention to the man behind the curtain!" If you define yourself as the problem and convince yourself that you wouldn't be feeling this way if you just had better boundaries and meditation habits, if only you were only more motivated or ambitious . . . if you do this you're more likely to put your head down and tolerate nonsense, while trying to "pull yourself up by your bootstraps," than to look outward and upward for accountability and change from the systems and people benefiting from your labor.

There are heavy, invisible hands pressing on all our shoulders: classism, racism, sexism, ableism. . . . If you write the weight off as normal, as general stress and fatigue, or just attribute it to some personal failing to push through, this makes you easier to exploit. And if you fail to understand how the weight compounds when layers of -isms pile on, this also makes you easier to polarize and distract. Unity and peaceful collective action are required to shift the systems keeping so many people exhausted and burnt out. But it feels harder to mobilize, act, and care for one another when we are exhausted and burnt out. And it's hard to remember that we are all interconnected as a human family when you are "in the zone," trying to feed your family. It's hard to stay in touch with the fact that life is simply bursting at the seams with beauty and mystery, everywhere you look, when you're so exhausted you can barely keep your eyes open on your commute home.

Finding your way back to yourself through burnout is a fundamentally revolutionary act. As is prioritizing rest and opting out of grind culture. It is critical to remember that our collective liberation does not call us to individually sacrifice everything at the altar of self-improvement. Sure, there are seasons when we must prioritize growth and work really intentionally to heal and evolve ourselves. But ceaseless self-improvement is just more perfectionism and grind culture. Loads of companies make millions annually because so many get convinced that they are not enough as they are, that they must purchase something to achieve enoughness. What does it feel like to try on this thought: *I'm enough, just as I am, even if I don't work any harder, even if I don't achieve everything expected of me—everything I expect of myself?*

Now that you've had some space to think through your personal risk factors that set you up for burnout, the next key offers you some opportunities to self-assess your current burnout and to survey how it uniquely shows up in you. One of the most common complaints I hear clients report is the sense that they know what to do to feel better, but (a) they feel too exhausted to do the things that help them feel better, and/or (b) by the time they recognize the signs it already feels too late. So, the next key offers ways to recognize burnout in yourself faster. Later on, as you continue to read farther into this book, you will notice lots of different tips and recommendations for what to do to move through burnout and feel better. And we've already begun, by increasing your understanding as you begin to identify and define the problem.

KEY 2

Recognize When You Are Careening Toward Burnout

> To pay attention is to love.
>
> —SHARON SALZBERG

As a mental health clinician, I notice clients frequently show up to therapy for burnout when they're already sizzled to a crisp, not before they burn out or when they are first beginning to careen toward it. The longer you stay stuck in burnout, the longer it generally takes to fully get back on the road to thriving. One of the trickiest things about burning out is that often when it's happening, the front part of your brain doesn't have enough fuel to run at full capacity. And that part of the brain does things like analysis, decision making, and planning into the future. Self-awareness is physically more challenging when you're burnt out because it's harder to keep your brain turned on and tuned in. It's incredibly common for clients to first show up to therapy for burnout months to years after they initially began experiencing burnout. But plenty can be done if you have already fully bottomed out into burnout—you'll just spend less money and time healing the sooner you get going. In my own field, I wish that we all received more information on prevention before getting thrown into training programs.

It is helpful to imagine a spectrum from fully burnt out to neutral to engaged/flourishing: from running on fumes, to half a tank of gas, to a full tank with a top off. Healing burnout isn't just about cutting stress out of life or reducing suffering—it's also about *adding* play, curiosity, wonder, moments of joy and excitement, feelings of pleasure, trust, and intimacy. Sometimes a stressor is inescapable (or inescapable for a season), and the best you can do is soothe and reassure yourself and those you love as you plot your activism and envision a world where people don't have to burn themselves out to keep themselves and their family fed or their community served. But sticking your head in the sand, telling everyone "I'm fine," and never taking anyone up on offers to help—though it may seem like a noble thing to do—in the long term, it will often unsettle more people and force you to ask for big help when things inevitably explode or start to come out sideways on people you love when you act from a place of frustration.

Throughout this book, I want to make sure to consistently speak to those of you dealing with burnout outside of a workplace or training context. Especially if you are a caregiver, it is incredibly common not to notice the careening toward burnout and to finally recognize it only in a more sudden—sometimes explosive—fashion. Many clients and friends describe it as a breakdown or meltdown, where you may feel forced into finally asking for help. I've been there myself! Recognizing when you're burning out, or about to, is an act of love and protection—not just for yourself, but for those around you who may depend on you. The sooner you intervene in your burnout, the less likely you'll be to lash out or react from a place of frustration. Anyone who has ever unintentionally snapped at a child, pet, or loved one knows what I'm talking about. Being able to stay in leadership of yourself through burnout can reduce the risk for harm and prevent abusive situations.

> **SIGNS OF CAREGIVER STRESS**
>
> - Feeling burdened or worrying all the time
> - Feeling tired often
> - Sleeping too much or not enough
> - Gaining or losing weight
> - Becoming easily irked or angry
> - Losing interest in activities you used to enjoy
> - Feeling sad
> - Having frequent headaches or other pains or health problems
> - Misusing alcohol or drugs, including prescription medicines
> - Missing your own medical appointments
>
> Source: (Mayo Clinic Staff, 2023, August 9)

This chapter will help you enhance your ability to recognize your unique burnout warning signs and self-assess with evidence-based tools. To get your burnout treated appropriately, it's important, first, to make sure that it is in fact burnout and, second, to rule out other conditions that can be mistaken for burnout, such as depression, anxiety, or undiagnosed autism or ADHD. In addition to thinking and feeling through your body, mind, and relationships when you're burning out, you will also begin to see what practical things you can do right now to support the start of your healing.

THEORY AND BACKGROUND

First let's get familiar with some of the language commonly used in scientific studies and literature about burnout. Fun fact: the first person to actually say "burnt out" was novelist Graham Greene, describing a fictional architect who had lost his ability to find pleasure in life or meaning in art in his 1960 book, *A Burnt-Out Case*. In the mid-1970s, German-born American psychologist Herbert Freudenberger (1974) was the first to professionally describe burnout. He classified it has having three aspects (pp. 159–165):

- *Emotional exhaustion*: "the fatigue that comes from caring too much for too long"
- *Depersonalization*: "the depletion of empathy, caring, and compassion"
- *Decreased sense of accomplishment*: "an unconquerable sense of futility: feeling that nothing you do makes any difference"

In 1981, just a year after Freudenberger and Géraldine Richelson (1980) published the first comprehensive research on the subject, Christina Maslach and Susan E. Jackson developed the Maslach Burnout Inventory (MBI) to assess an individual's level of burnout, which is still widely used today (Maslach & Jackson, 1981). The MBI comprises 22 items: nine measure emotional exhaustion, five measure depersonalization ("impaired and distorted perception of oneself, of others and one's environment . . . [that] manifests . . . as an affective-symptomatic lack of empathy"; Prinz et al. 2012), and eight measure (reduced) personal accomplishment. Burnout in these three dimensions involves

- Increased feelings of emotional exhaustion (depleted psychological resources)
- Development of negative, cynical attitudes and feelings toward clients/patients/students (callous, even dehumanized perception of other can lead to view clients as deserving of troubles)
- Tendency to evaluate oneself negatively, particularly with regard to one's work with clients (feeling unhappy about self and dissatisfied with accomplishments on the job)

In 2019, the World Health Organization updated the International Classification of Diseases, Eleventh Revision (ICD-11) with the following definition:

> Burnout is a syndrome conceptualized as resulting from chronic workplace stress that has not been successfully managed. It is characterized by three dimensions: (1) feelings of energy depletion or exhaustion; (2) increased mental distance from one's job, or feelings of negativism or cynicism related to one's job; and (3) a sense of ineffectiveness and lack of accomplishment. Burn-out refers specifically to phenomena in the occupational context and should not be applied to describe experiences in other areas of life. (World Health Organization, 2019)

Please note that for the purposes of this book, caregiving and parenting are considered to be within the occupational context, regardless of involving unpaid labor outside a workplace. Here, failing to include this type of work leaves out a lot of people who can benefit from the ideas and activities in this book.

Now that you've had a chance to look through some of the scientific definitions, what rings true for you personally? After just initially reading through some definitions, are you suspecting that you are currently burnt out? Burning out? Already absolute burnt toast? The good news is that, collectively, our human family is beginning to push back (or at least envision how to) on the work conditions (e.g., 40+ hour work weeks, lack of paid time off) and cultural norms (e.g., grind-and-hustle culture) that our systems have rewarded and advanced for decades.

FIGURE 2.1
Summary Timeline

1974 — Herbert Freudenberger defines burnout (Freudenberger, 1974).

1980 — Freudenberger and Richelson publish comprehensive burnout study (Freudenberger & Richelson, 1980).

1981 — Maslach and Jackson create the MBI (Maslach & Jackson, 1981).

1980s — Charles Figley studies compassion fatigue: "The deep physical, emotional, and spiritual exhaustion that can result from working day to day in an intense caregiving environment" (Figley & Roop, 2006).

1986 — Maslach and Jackson distinguish three dimensions of burnout: emotional exhaustion, cynicism or depersonalization, and diminished sense of personal accomplishment (Maslach & Jackson, 1981).

1992 — Joinson coins the phrase *compassion fatigue* to describe "loss of the ability to nurture" in nursing professionals (Joinson, 1992).

2010 — Beth Hudnall Stamm introduces the Professional Quality of Life Measure (ProQOL; Stamm, 2010).

2019 — Mayo Clinic defines *burnout* as "a state of physical, emotional and mental exhaustion accompanied by doubts about one's competence and the value of one's work" (Mayo Clinic, 2023).

2019 — World Health Organization recognizes burnout in the International Classification of Diseases, Eleventh Revision (ICD-11) (World Health Organization, 1993).

Credit: Stoewen (2019), Schaufeli (2017), Leone et al. (2011)

DISCOVERING THE KEY

As a clinician I've noticed that it's incredibly common for clients to write burnout symptoms off as "just stress" or mere physical exhaustion that a good nap or vacation could resolve. If you still aren't feeling sure if what you've been experiencing is exhaustion, anxiety, depression, and/or burnout, I recommend checking in with your mental health provider, or hiring one for the first time, to help you get some clarity. We are all part of the same human family, so of course everyone will have some things in common. At the same time, how burnout shows up in each person is *incredibly* unique. Over the last few years, I've compiled a list of phrases that clients and students have used to describe their emotional experience of burnout. This might be especially soothing to read if you feel "crazy" for feeling how you feel, or like you somehow don't make sense. Yes, you are unique, but you also are not alone—you are a part of a larger, interconnected family.

Please note: Before reading the list below, take a moment to think of an image or a metaphor that comes up for you when you think about what burnout feels like for you. What image comes to your mind when you think about burnout?

Common Responses to "What Does Burnout Feel Like?"

- Drowning/sinking/swimming against a current or upstream
- Being carried away down raging rapids or lost out at sea
- Taking on water and bailing it out just enough to keep barely afloat
- Being stuck in a cave or at the bottom of the sea, or lost in a desert
- Suffocating/not being able to breathe (or breathe fully out), being smothered
- "Dream punching/running" (feeling you put a lot of effort and it doesn't do anything)

- Extreme gravity/being physically weighed down
- Digging a hole while someone periodically dumps more sand in
- "Running a car on a gallon of gas a day—never filling up, always running out"
- Becoming a robot or machine, "human parts unplugged"
- A void or black hole, a "shell of myself," a hollow tree
- Asleep or in a dream (or nightmare), a zombie or ghost
- Performer on stage or wearing a mask

Do any of these feel familiar? Which stand out to you the most? Do some resonate more in certain contexts or at different times of day than others?

Please note: It is critical to remember that, although we can assess for common features of burnout, every person feels and describes it differently. The key is really getting to know your body and yourself at a deeper level so that you can catch yourself *before* you slip and fall all the way into burnout. There will also be times when you are so busy and overwhelmed that you don't actually even notice you are burning out. This chapter will help you think through reaching out to someone you trust who could be an accountability partner. The following activities also offer opportunities to explore how burnt out you are and to recognize what it feels like when you're *not* burnt out—when you're in your "core-self" energy. You will create your own danger rating chart, so you can practice recognizing the signs and symptoms and getting the support you need before things really go off the rails.

AUTISTIC BURNOUT

It's also important to name that it's common for neurodiverse people (e.g., on the autism spectrum and/or diagnosed with ADHD) and those with chronic and terminal conditions to experience burnout even if they aren't employed or in a traditional role. "Autistic burnout," for example, is real and valid. "Autistic burnout appears to be a phenomenon distinct from occupational burnout or clinical depression" (Raymaker et al., 2020, pp. 132–143). Scientist, artist, and activist Dora Raymaker and colleagues (2020) defined autistic burnout as "a syndrome conceptualized as resulting from chronic life stress and a mismatch of expectations and abilities without adequate supports. It is characterized by pervasive, long-term (typically 3 or more months) exhaustion, loss of function, and reduced tolerance to stimulus."

Examples of ways that Raymaker et al.'s participants reported relieving and preventing their autistic burnout include interacting with others who accept them for who they were, attending to autistic needs like stimming or pursuing special interests, receiving reasonable adjustments at school or work, physical support like someone bringing groceries over, and learning how to set boundaries and self-advocate, as well as self-knowledge, or learning to recognize early signs of autistic burnout. The act of masking autistic traits is kind of like playing music on your phone but turning the volume off—the battery just slowly gets drained even though you aren't enjoying any tunes. If you're neurotypical but you experience chronic pain and/or fatigue, this way of conceptualizing burnout can help you too!

ACTIVITY 2A
Maslach Burnout Inventory (MBI)

As you become clearer about who you really are, you'll be better able to decide what is best for you—the first time around.

—OPRAH WINFREY

Goal

To briefly estimate your current level of burnout, differentiate it from regular exhaustion, and plan a way(s) to reassess in 6 months and again at 1 year to track your progress as you set out to navigate your way back from burnout.

Instructions

First, please read through the factors below used to measure burnout in the MBI. Next, complete the subsequent prompts, and then complete the checklist that follows.

Please note: This activity is an informal approach to assessing burnout. While it may be useful to you, it has not been validated through controlled scientific tests, so it cannot be used as an official diagnostic technique. If you'd like to purchase and complete a rigorously researched and validated tool to assess your level of burnout, you can complete the "MBI-GS," or Maslach Burnout Inventory—General Survey, which you can find at https://www.mindgarden.com/312-mbi-general-survey.

Factors

1. Exhaustion: feelings of being overextended and exhausted by one's work
2. Cynicism: an indifference or a distant attitude towards your work
3. Professional Efficacy: satisfaction with past and present accomplishments, and an individual's expectations of continued effectiveness at work

Prompts

> How exhausted do you feel? Have you noticed a significant increase in exhaustion? Cynicism?
>
> For how long have you felt this exhaustion and cynicism? Have you ever felt this before? If yes, when? What was the ultimate outcome?
>
> When you're feeling cynical or hopeless/helpless, what are the thoughts that you have? (For example, *I'm no good*, or *Everyone sucks*, or *This is pointless*, or *Humans are mostly terrible*). What main story or stories do you tell about what's happening?
>
> How satisfied have you been feeling lately with your present-day achievements and past accomplishments at work? How effective do you estimate yourself to be? Compared to when you first began in your role/responsibility? Does it feel like you've grown? Reached your potential?

Checklist: Please put a check mark beside each statement below that feels true for you. The more statements that feel true, the more likely it is you're experiencing burnout.

- ❏ More days than not, I feel exhausted and/or emotionally drained.
- ❏ I generally feel overextended by daily activities required of me.
- ❏ More weeks than not, daily tasks I must do get in the way of my social and family life.
- ❏ I've been feeling more indifferent, distant, even cynical toward daily activities required of me.
- ❏ I feel like I'm becoming less effective and competent at my daily tasks.
- ❏ Nothing I do really seems to matter—I can't change the daily activities required of me no matter what I do.

- ❑ I worry I'm becoming insensitive to the people/clients/patients I serve/help/care for.
- ❑ I've had less patience lately than usual.
- ❑ I wake up in the morning feeling exhausted and already negative about the day.

___ **Total** (the more items you mark true, the more likely it is you're burnt out)

Relational Activity Add-On: Ask a trusted friend, coworker, colleague, supervisor, or mentor how you seem to them at work lately. Are they worried at all that you might be burning out in your role? You could also ask a partner or spouse if you work in the home.

ACTIVITY 2B
Recognize Your "Core-Self" Energy

> Find out who you are and do it on purpose.
>
> —DOLLY PARTON

Goal
To identify the feelings and sensations of embodying *core-self energy* (calm, curious, clear, compassionate, confident, courageous, creative, connected), to increase ability to recognize imbalance and burnout, and to learn about the ventral vagal state of feeling "grounded."

Instructions
Please take a look at Richard Schwartz's list of the "Eight Cs of Self" (from family systems therapy) below (Schwartz, 2021, p. 6). First, rate each quality from 1 to 10, with 10 being "I strongly agree that feel this way lately," 5 being "I sometimes feel this way lately," and 1 being "I rarely/never feel this lately." (I invite you to use a sticky note or a notes

app in your phone to document your scores, as opposed to writing in the book. This way, you can measure again in 6 months and 1 year to track your progress.) Then, answer the prompts that follow related to a recent time when experienced these feelings.

CALM	_____
CURIOUS	_____
CLEAR/CLARITY	_____
COMPASSIONATE	_____
CONFIDENT	_____
COURAGEOUS	_____
CREATIVE	_____
CONNECTED	_____

When do you feel the calmest? The least calm?

When do you feel the most curious? The least?

When do you feel the clearest or have the most clarity? The least?

When do you feel the most compassionate? The least?

When do you feel the most confident? The least?

When do you feel the most courageous? The least?

When do you feel the most creative? The least?

When do you feel the most connected? The least?

Think of a time when you felt most or all of the Eight Cs at once. When was it? What was it like?

When you're upset, exhausted, and/or stressed out, which of the Eight Cs goes away the fastest? (For example, "When I get triggered and I'm already stressed, my curiosity is the first thing to go out the window—I know everything, it's black-and-white, and you're wrong.")

Which of the Eight Cs might serve as barometers to help signal you are starting to burn out? (For example, "I can tell that I'm beginning to burn out when my level of compassion drops drastically," or, "If I suddenly question everything—nothing seems clear anymore—that's often a sign I'm already seriously burned.")

Think about your daily responsibilities. How much of the time do you get to really feel like your true, whole self—all of the Eight Cs—during the day?

If you feel up for it, choose one thing that you could be intentional about including in your weekly routine that allows you to access this core-self energy. It might be something you used to enjoy that just fell out of habit, or it could be a new skill or hobby you've been eyeing. What day of the week has the most wiggle room for this idea? Looking at your calendar, specifically when will you carve out a little time to do it?

If you have a work persona or mask that you put on for work or for people outside of your immediate family and close friends, how would you describe it? Does it take energy for you to do this? When your battery feels drained, how do you recharge?

Brainstorm for a moment and begin to make a specific plan to intentionally do something at least once a week (for at least 5–20 minutes) so that you feel the Eight Cs. What could you try? Who might you need to recruit for help, childcare, and so forth?

Relational Activity Add-On: Ask your partner, friend, loved-one, or mentor when they think you are "most yourself." What do you notice as you listen to their response?

ACTIVITY 2C
My Burnout Danger Rating

> Don't be afraid to ask questions. Don't be afraid to ask for help when you need it. I do that every day. Asking for help isn't a sign of weakness, it's a sign of strength. If shows you have the courage to admit when you don't know something, and to learn something new.
>
> —BARACK OBAMA

Goal
To create a scale from low to catastrophic and begin to identify some specific behaviors, thoughts, and feelings you can use as warning signs that indicate when you need to make a change, ask for help or delegate, and/or engage in self-care or community care.

Instructions
Below is a risk-level warning sign like they use for fire danger ratings, with levels low, moderate, high, extreme, and catastrophic.

A) Please list some of the thoughts you're likely to be thinking at each level. If you need help getting started, try the prompt: "When I'm at ____ level, the story I'm telling myself is ____."

Example Risk Levels

LOW RISK: "I've got this. It doesn't have to be perfect. I can figure this out—I can get help."

MODERATE RISK: "If I have to get help I guess I can—but I should be able on my own."

HIGH RISK: "Don't give up. It will just get better with time. Don't stop. Keep going."

FIGURE 2.2
Risk-Level Warning Sign

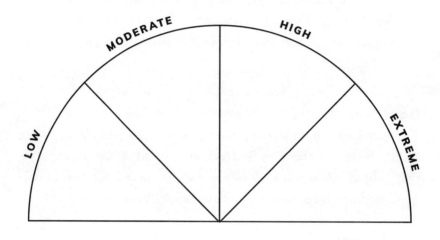

EXAMPLE

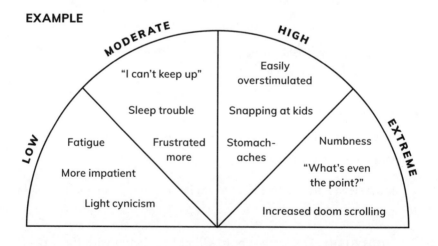

EXTREME RISK: "I'm the only one who can hold this together. It all falls apart if I give up."

CATASTROPHIC RISK: "Oh no. Everything is ruined. It's completely hopeless—I'm so screwed."

B) Please imagine what feels like the *opposite* of burnout to you—not just a neutral feeling or the absence of daily terror, but thriving and flourishing. Notice if it's easy or difficult to imagine this. Does trying to envision this stir up any emotions? It if feels safe, make room for whatever is coming up for you. It's normal for this question to surface some deep grief, longing, even rage. It's also normal if you feel like you can't even allow yourself to imagine an alternate reality—harsher and hopeless parts of ourselves often team up and chime in: "What's even the point? It's impossible. It feels masochistic to allow myself to think of an ideal dream scenario. It's so beyond out of my reach."

> When you imagine yourself not burnt out but flourishing, what comes to mind? What do you see? What is your attitude like? What is the environment around you like?
>
> What's different about your present-day self and situation compared with the flourishing version of you that you envisioned? What seem like blocks or barriers in the way of the dream happening?

C) Draw your own burnout danger rating scale and make note of some behaviors, emotions/feelings, and physical sensations/symptoms you'd be likely to experience at each level.

Below are brief lists of some common behaviors, emotions or feelings, and physical sensations and symptoms in case you need help putting this into words.

Example Behaviors/Symptoms

- Body-focused repetitive behaviors, such as trichotillomania (compulsive hair pulling), dermatillomania (compulsive skin picking), onychophagia (nail-biting)
- Distract by staying excessively busy and overbooked outside of work
- Express frustration in an angry way, such as snapping or yelling
- Emotionally withdraw
- Numb out with activities (e.g., scrolling phone, gaming, binge eating, television/media consumption)
- Increase substance use (e.g., alcohol, opioids, cocaine, ketamine, MDMA, cannabis)
- Intellectualize instead of allowing yourself to feel emotions (e.g., only read books to learn about burnout without actually allowing yourself to really feel the sadness, rage, guilt)
- Isolate, socially disconnect, or shut others out
- Lose interest in people, places, and/or activities you used to enjoy (e.g., hobbies, art, extracurriculars)
- Overuse exercise
- Run away (e.g., give your 2 weeks' notice or actually pack up and move away, or just jump in the car and drive off at the first whiff of conflict)
- Take on a savior or martyr role
- Sensory-seeking behaviors, such as thrill seeking or risk taking (e.g., gambling, driving unsafely or "joyrides," having unplanned sex without implementing safer sex practices)
- Sleeping too much or not enough
- Vent to anyone who will listen to an excessive degree

Example Emotions/Feelings

- Afraid
- Agitated
- Betrayed
- Bored
- Burnt out
- Calm
- Confused
- Depressed
- Disgusted
- Distressed
- Empty
- Exhausted
- Frazzled
- Guilty
- Happy
- Hopeful
- Hopeless
- Listless
- Lonely
- Lost
- Moved
- Nervous
- Numb
- Overstimulated
- Overwhelmed

Example Physical Sensations/Symptoms

- Aches and pain, soreness, chronic pain
- Digestion, stomach issues
- Dissociation, feeling "foggy" or "far away" from yourself
- Fatigue, feeling sleepy even when waking after adequate rest
- Gastrointestinal discomfort
- Intensified menstrual and premenstrual symptoms
- Irregular and/or disturbed sleep
- Jaw tightness/pain
- Lump in the throat
- Memory issues
- Migraines or headaches

- Nocturnal bruxism (tooth-grinding)
- Numbness, tingling
- Pelvic pain
- Racing heart or panic attacks
- Skin issues (e.g., hives, eczema, acne)
- Temperature change (e.g., cold, hot, clammy, sweaty)
- Tightness

Please note: If you're in a relationship or friendship, it can be helpful for your partner or friend to fill out your rating scale and go over your responses together. Sometimes they will notice something helpful that's tricky to notice without them.

> ### IS MY SUBSTANCE USE PROBLEMATIC?
>
> If you're wondering if your alcohol or drug use is problematic, or someone has tried to tell you it is, that can be a sign it's worth reaching out to explore what resources are accessible and available to you. Another question that can be helpful to ask yourself: "Am I using/drinking/taking ___ (your substance of choice) to get out of the red and back into the black? Am I already in a deficit when I add the substance/s? Or am I solid and in the black before I choose to add a substance to enhance my experience and access joyfulness?" If it feels like you need the substance in order to feel good—a necessity, not a novelty—it can be worth checking in with a mental health professional.
>
> If you aren't sure where to begin, the Substance Abuse and Mental Health Services Administration (SAMHSA) can help with treatment location. You can visit their website at

> http://www.samhsa.gov, and they also have a free, confidential helpline: 1-(800)-662-HELP (4357), as well as a ton of other resources.
>
> I also want to invite you to treat yourself gently and give yourself as much grace as you can—it's *incredibly* common for people to try to cope with feelings of loneliness, pain, grief, and powerlessness by numbing out or distracting from the pain with substances. You're human. You're not alone. And there's help.

ACTIVITY 2D
Accountability Partners

> Loving ourselves and each other deepens our disruption of the dominant systems. They want us unwell, fearful, exhausted, and without deep self-love because you are easier to manipulate when you are distracted by what is not real or true.
>
> —TRICIA HERSEY

> You don't have to worry about burning bridges if you're building your own.
>
> —KERRY E. WAGNER

Goal

To think through selecting an accountability partner(s) and/or community (e.g., therapist, coworker, mommy group friend, burnout support group) and to make a plan for regular, honest check-ins and giving people radical permission to insist we care for ourselves, accept help, or say no—whatever we know we need that feels challenging to achieve.

Instructions

Please read through and complete the prompts below.

Who is a trusted person/people in your life you can share with without feeling guilty (e.g., a therapist, spiritual leader, consultation or support group, coworker who vents and listens in a healthy balance that feels mutual and energy giving)? If you can't think of anyone, what does it feel like sitting with that?

Does this person already know they're your person? What makes you think so or not? (For example, "Yes; it's my work-wife. I think so because we have matching shirts and a friendship bracelet." Or, "Yes; I pay them—they're my therapist.")

Right now, does it feel like there are any factors (e.g., pregnancy, recent loss or death in the family) that might make it unreasonable to ask them to provide emotional support? If yes, I trust your gut about not seeking/relying on support from them in this season. If you are unsure if someone is available to emotionally support you, what would it sound like to check in with them about their bandwidth and give grace and permission to say no? (For example, "Hey, love, I know you've got a lot going on. Wondering if you'd be interested in an accountability partner—I think we could help each other be kinder to ourselves. No worries at all if you don't have the bandwidth.")

What ways do you respond best to if someone is trying to check in on your well-being? (For example, "I prefer a quick, 'You good?' with eye contact, especially with close friends and coworkers. My bestie and I even have a special thumbs-up gesture that we use to check in on each other if we aren't supposed to be chatting." Or "I really love when my colleague texts, 'Thinking about you! I know you're slammed right now but I would love to get on your schedule if you've got an opening coming up. Here are some dates that work for me. . . '") We all have different preferences when it comes to receiving care, so make sure that everyone knows what *actually helps* you feel heard and understood, soothed and reassured. Make sure to communicate your preferences with your accountability partner/group so that your needs get met and no one wastes energy trying to offer something that you don't actually need.

If your accountability partner is a friend or coworker/colleague, how can you let each other know if someone's venting is starting to veer into therapy territory? How can you bring this up while also being mindful of anyone who may get triggered if they feel like a burden, for instance? Make agreements with each other how you will let each other know if it ever feels like something being shared might be better shared with a therapist or with the person they're venting about, especially if it gets to feeling perpetual and nonstop.

EVALUATE AND PLAN TO USE THIS KEY (OR NOT!)

Below are some prompts you can use to evaluate and plan.

> How was this second key for you? Any new knowledge or understandings? Any bits or parts you really connected with or liked? Anything you'd like to immediately return to sender?
>
> What I took from this key and the activities was really that ___ (summarize). (For example, "I can recognize when I'm beginning to burn out and get help before I fully bottom out into burnout.")
>
> My specific plan for how I'll use this key is ___ (e.g., "I'll chat with my best friend at work and see if she wants to talk about our boundaries and how we can look out for each other and have each other's backs while we're interns").

What's your plan before you move on to the next chapter? Needing anything? Often during the initial assessment phase of therapy, there can be a sense of annoyance or readiness to move from awareness and understanding into action. Do you need to reassure a problem-solver or solution-focused part of you that you're going to also be addressing action items? If you're feeling impatient or antsy, please feel invited to let your body move around a bit before continuing on. This is really normal if you suspected you were burnt out, but didn't really want to fully acknowledge it. Clients often report that it can feel overwhelming to admit being burnt out because they're already exhausted, and the idea of having to do something more for healing is just too much. If you're feeling this sort of overwhelm, it might help to journal a bit about it to get it off your chest, or to chat with someone you trust who will validate and support you without trying to rush into action.

FINAL THOUGHTS

When you are in distress, you need practical solutions, not just awareness and explanations. As you continue through this book, you will find plenty of opportunities to understand the underlying whys and how you got there. I'd like to warn those of you who also overthink and intellectualize in order to avoid feelings: it can be easy to get so caught up in trying to get to insight and deep understanding of a problem that you don't *act*. And it's so common to try to grab for explanations and understanding when we are least able to think super clearly or existentially—when we're at our most stressed. My invitation to you is to focus more on how you are feeling in the present and how efficiently and comfortably you can shift from stress and feelings of disconnection to feelings of safety and connection (as opposed to getting bogged down in trying to understand why everything is the way it is right out the gate).

There will be plenty of time as you move toward healing and

flourishing to begin to really make sense of things—to trace the roots all the way down into your personal story, and beyond to the generations before you. In fact, you'll be better equipped to use your brain to think more deeply and existentially once you've made some space and started to feel more stabilized—more yourself. While everyone's path back from burnout looks different, it can help to try to proceed in an order like this:

1. "I wonder if I'm burnt out?"
2. "What risk factors and symptoms do I have?"
3. "I am burnt out."
4. "What are solutions for immediate relief?"
5. "Why am I burnt out?"
6. "What needs to be built into my rhythms and routines to help with long-term protection?"

Repeat as needed, from the top.

I share because it's normal for impatient parts of ourselves to show up during assessment. If you're at this point feeling like, "Okay, duh, I'm burnt out—but what do I *do*?" then keep reading! Now that you've had some space to think about the definition of burnout and how you can tell when you're experiencing it, the next chapter will help you think through when it's appropriate to attempt to slow or step back, and when you need to walk away or quit. One of the most common complaints I hear from clients is that they aren't sure whether leaving or stepping back at work is necessary to heal. Even just considering the thought of resigning or changing positions, roles, or careers can feel scary. We will practice zooming out to consider the bigger picture and what best serves you and thinking through possible options.

KEY 3

Learn When and How to Slow Down, Step Back, or Walk Away

> We must believe that we are worthy of rest. We don't have to earn it.
> It is our birthright. It is one of our most ancient and primal needs.
>
> —TRICIA HERSEY

Just to start off, I want to assure you that I'm not going to tell you that you should just quit your job—I hear some version of this worry from so many clients as we're kicking off therapy. If you are a parent or caregiver, as an obvious example, that may actually not be an option. This chapter is about possibilities. I find that so often more possibilities exist than people can easily see. And when you're burnt out, it's like trying to balance a complex equation while looking through a kaleidoscope.

I also want to say that if, somewhere deep inside, you feel like you might need to reconsider things in a big way, you are deserving of the time and support needed to sort through all that. If this all feels like too overwhelming of a thought to even begin to wade into, that's okay. When I'm most burnt out, I get so stubborn and fixated on whatever my goal is—I can remember telling others to get out of my face with any notions of quitting or slowing my pace. Often, I didn't even perceive it as being about *me*—it sounded like, "I can't quit! If

I quit, everyone staying behind here will just be left living an even worse nightmare."

I also bring this up because I want to assure you that I'm not here to give you advice. Perhaps that sounds odd, because this is a self-help book, but I don't know you personally. I don't know your story, what you've lived through—what your ancestors lived through. I don't know better than you. I *can* promise that I won't pretend like everyone can just do the same cookie-cutter things to rest, address burnout, and experience relief and healing. If you don't have the option of stepping back or slowing down—or you won't for some time—I'm still going to give you some practical, low-effort ways to feel better. Just know you can skip forward to the activities and feel invited to engage at whatever level feels comfortable right now.

Key 3 is about finding ways feel more restored and rested. It's about figuring out what you can do to create some space and peace amidst the chaos, to take a beat and breathe out. Sometimes you have the ability to slow down or change pace, and other times there's not as much choice or control and you *do* have to keep on keeping on and focus on finding ways to keep the wheels from falling off. Since the 1980s, burnout treatment efforts have tended to focus on training patients in techniques to manage stress and reduce anxiety, but research shows that these types of techniques alone do little to improve symptoms. While we know that self-care alone doesn't fix burnout, you do need some kind of solid foundation with self-care practices and routines that support your body, brain, mind, and relationships. In terms of self-care, because of what the research shows, Key 3 focuses mainly on rest, downtime, and sleep hygiene. You'll also think through some topics such as boundary setting and asking for help.

You'll begin by learning the evidence from research on what it takes to keep a human brain healthy. Then, you can effectively use your healthy brain to evaluate whether you are best served by staying in your current work environment/role, stepping back or requesting a change in contract or accommodations, or leaving or making a plan to leave in the future, if it's not currently an option. Even if you are not able to get space from what's stressing you out the most, working to keep your brain healthy will help you feel better in the midst of the struggle. What it really comes down to is this: It is possible to do all the things shown to help with burnout, but at the end of the day, if you are surrounded by people misusing or abusing their power who benefit from exploiting you and have no motivation to change their behavior, then it is unlikely you will feel really successful at preventing or reversing burnout.

THEORY AND BACKGROUND

Ask a therapist or burnout researcher what the actual best way to heal burnout is, and a top—if not *the* top—response will be to step away from the stressor(s): "Take a break." This answer can be enormously frustrating for people experiencing burnout primarily because of their kids, mental or physical condition, a sick family member, or another situation that cannot be abandoned. Annoyingly, though, the simplest solution to burnout seems to be to increase the amount of space or distance between you and what's burning you out—to detach more. Across professions right now, though, burnout is at an all-time high and is only exacerbated by such things as the politicization of mask wearing and other unrelenting stressors (Abramson, 2022). Long story short, you can trust that corporate entities are pouring tons of funding into finding ways to "help" (i.e., get more out of their employees).

Burnout researchers Kira Schabram, Matt Bloom, and DJ DiDonna studied break-taking in 2023. They found that just taking a vacation—a go-to for people burning out—isn't going to cure your burnout, but taking a more extended time off can actually help. One recommendation they make is to plan and take a sabbatical, an extended break from your job that's actually long enough for you to truly distance yourself from your normal work life. One of my professors in grad school had come from practicing in New York City, where therapists mostly can't be found during the months of July and December. He gave me the idea of a month-long sabbatical, which I still take every July. Obviously not everyone has the freedom and ability to take time off from work regularly, or at all, so know that this is just one tool that can help with burnout. If it's possible for you, I can't recommend it enough.

Schabram et al. (2023) noted:

> We discover that sabbaticals combine "building blocks"—distinct periods dedicated to *recover*, *explore*, or *practice*—into three typical trajectories: *working holidays* (alternating recovery and practice), *free dives* (alternating recovery and exploration), and *quests* (unfolding from recovery to exploration to practice). (pp. 441–468)

Looking at participants in the study, they found those on working holidays tended to return to their usual lives, but they had increased confidence and more of a need for balance. The "free divers" ended up pursuing similar but better-fitting work, such as switching companies or employers or positions. The "questers" were most likely to go ahead and make a massive career change.

One more bit of science, if you are not already familiar with the term *sleep hygiene*, coined by Peter Hauri (1996) to describe what patients can do to eliminate factors interfering with sleep. The activities section explores more about better sleep. The main thing to know—which will not shock you—is that research shows that insufficient/disturbed sleep is a "critically important risk factor for burnout" (Kancherla et al., 2020, p. 807), predicts burnout (Söderström et al., 2012), and makes burnout worse (Pagnin et al., 2014). And all sorts of factors complicate this. Stress and health researchers Sharon Toker and Samuel Melamed (2017, pp. 168–185) found that "long work hours, a lack of boundaries between work and nonwork time, and work–home interference . . . impede recovery processes and . . . increase the risk of fatigue and burnout." I share this because it can help with hopelessness about recovery to know that, even if you can't completely control your time, you're not out of luck—boundary work can also help bring relief.

> **PRACTICING SAYING "NO"**
>
> If you're someone who struggles to say no and unwittingly ends up overextending yourself, it can take some practice to feel more comfortable with letting others know you can't help.
>
> *Tip:* Let those you're closest with know that you are working on saying no to protect your energy level. (You can also do this with asking for help or even delegating.) Let them know what helps make it easier for you to feel comfortable declining an invitation or request for help (e.g., "I still like to be invited even though I have to decline a lot right now; it helps me to know you won't stop inviting me all together if sometimes I need to decline," or "It helps me if I hear you say something like 'no pressure' or 'there'll be another chance.'").
>
> *Please note:* Recruit someone to support you with this *only* if you sense they have the capacity/ability to hear your no and to honor it without making you feel bad or trying to change your mind.

DISCOVERING THE KEY

My own path to my devotion to rest, sleep, naps, and taking breaks and time off was quite spiritual, so it almost feels odd to start with hard science like I just did. In the introduction I mentioned Tricia Hersey's manifesto, *Rest Is Resistance*. Before her book came out, she was a beloved figure on social media known as the "Nap Bishop" at the Nap Ministry. Her organization offers "collective napping experiences," where sacred spaces are set up for the community to nap together, and they create artful installations focused on the sacredness of rest.

An important distinction I feel like I can't overstate: resting for the purpose of being more productive is not the same as resting because you simply deserve to rest. Hersey (2022) says it better:

> The Rest Is Resistance framework . . . does not believe in the toxic idea that we are resting to recharge and rejuvenate so we can be prepared to give more output to capitalism. What we have internalized as productivity has been informed by a capitalist, ableist, patriarchal system. Our drive and obsession to always be in a state of "productivity" leads us to the path of exhaustion, guilt, and shame. We falsely believe we are not doing enough and that we must always be guiding our lives toward more labor. The distinction that must be repeated as many times as necessary is this: We are not resting to be productive. We are resting simply because it is our divine right to do so. (p. 11)

I, and many clients I've served, couldn't really get satisfying traction or forward motion toward healing until time was spent discovering and connecting with a sense of self-worth, as well as worthiness. Recovering from burnout takes effort! It's much easier to get on board if you front-load you efforts with some introspection and reassurance for your internal part who, however faintly, says, *I am worthy, I am deserving*. And, I can assure you that, if you have not yet arrived at a sense of worthiness, the path you're on right now will give you loads of chances to cultivate self-love. Loving and being loved by others also helps fill this cup. But if all this feels a bit too "out there" for you, don't worry—you will still find some useful tips and ideas.

I'll admit that, for me, I felt initially way more motivated to care for myself because my health and wellness impacts other vulnerable people. I certainly did not come to this work thinking, "I will take care of myself out of deep love and respect for myself." Instead, it was pragmatic at first: It was about surviving to be able to persist in helping. And the same went for boundaries and protecting myself. Finally, a mentor suggested that boundaries aren't just for protecting ourselves but also for protecting *others* from our aggression. If you feel the same, you're normal. And if you grew up in an environment where you repeatedly got the message that you don't matter, it may take intentional effort, such as counseling or group therapy, to really buy into how deeply you deserve care and comfort. Conversations around burnout can deepen significantly when this topic is front and center.

When I polled my audience on social media, asking what things are typically left out of books and resources for burnout, these were some of the most common responses:

- How to manage/heal when you still have to keep moving forward and working (e.g., financially you cannot afford to quit; you have to complete a training program that lasts years before you can move on; you're a caregiver and also have to work)
- How to take care of yourself when time and financial resources are tight
- How certain types of neurodiversity make you more likely to burn out, and what one can do in an inflexible and/or unjust work environment

I can't tell you how many clients get told some dismissive version of, "Why don't you *just* take a break?" While it is true that the most straightforward way to heal burnout is to step back and get distance from the stressor(s), this is not incredibly helpful advice to someone who can't or isn't ready to do that. Which people in our society are best able to slow down and step back from work if needed? Who has the option to fully walk away? Who has to have another job lined up before they can even think about it? The more resources you have, the easier it is to be cavalier about these decisions. Of course, I'm not saying that everyone who has wealth is easily able to rest, heal, and manage burnout—it takes *work* to manage burnout, no matter who you are.

In broad strokes, generally the more privilege and power you have, the more you'll probably hear me advocate for a serious slowdown, sabbatical(s), or a pause/stop, because clinically that's what my most trusted colleagues and I see generally helping most. I am aware that it takes financial stability to be able to choose to walk away from a job. I believe everyone should have more paid time off and the ability to take sabbaticals or more extended leaves of absence—it shouldn't be true, but as it stands, these are privileges. In my view, until legislative changes like fair wages and comprehensive health care come our way, we have to do the best we can with what we have. Further, those of us with more privilege (and less history of systemic oppression) have more responsibility to advocate for the changes we all need so that all of us may live joyfully and free from burnout. I work hard to manage my own burnout in large part so that I have enough energy to advocate for others drowning on levels I can only imagine from talking to so many burnt-out people. Regardless of your current context, the activities here will help you expand how you think about the care and keeping of you. If you've got the bandwidth now, you'll also get a chance to be honest with yourself about what's really right for you.

ACTIVITY 3A
Healthy Mind Platter

> Burnout is a slow, insidious experience. Burnout is not afraid of playing the long game. To prevent burnout, we need to play a long game too.
>
> —SALLY CLARKE

Goal

To familiarize yourself with interpersonal neurobiologist Dan Siegel's "Healthy Mind Platter," a research-based tool for maintaining optimal brain health, and to self-assess and think through ways to optimize the health of your brain matter (Siegel, n.d.).

Instructions

Take a moment to look over the Healthy Mind Platter. Then, read the descriptions below from Dan Siegel's website (Siegel, n.d.) and list some examples of ways you can engage in each category in your own life, given your unique abilities, interests, resources and opportunities.

Please note: The goal here is to aim for, "More days that not in a week, I meet these needs," not to do every single one of these every single day without fail.

Sleep time: "When we give the brain the rest it needs, we consolidate learning and recover from the experiences of the day" (e.g., sleeping, taking naps).

Physical time: "When we move our bodies, aerobically if medically possible, we strengthen the brain in many ways" (e.g., joyful movement, strength training, running club).

Focus time: "When we closely focus on tasks in a goal-oriented way, we take on challenges that make deep connections in the brain" (e.g., crossword puzzle, sudoku, aspects of work).

Connecting time: "When we connect with other people, ideally in person, and when we take time to appreciate our connection in the natural world around us, we activate and reinforce the brain's relational circuitry."

Playtime: "When we allow ourselves to be spontaneous or creative, playfully enjoying novel experiences, we help make new connections in the brain" (e.g., games, crafting, play with kids, engaging in a special interest even if it may look like work to someone neurotypical).

Downtime: "When we are non-focused, without any specific goal, and let our mind wander or simply relax, we can help the brain recharge" (e.g., sitting outside with the dog, watching a movie).

Time in: "When we quietly reflect internally, focusing on sensations, images, feelings and thoughts, we help to better integrate the brain" (e.g., mindfulness, meditation, body-centered somatic practices). (*Brain integration* refers to different parts of the brain working together harmoniously.)

ACTIVITY 3B
Big Breaks and Little Rests

> If you don't schedule a break, your body will take one for you. And it probably won't be at a convenient time.
>
> —UNKNOWN

Goal
To move beyond perfectionism and black-and-white thinking with respect to improving rest and to explore some different pathways to rest and recovery.

Instructions
Look over the types of sabbaticals below, from Schabram et al. (2023). Then, complete the prompts that follow.

Main Types of Sabbaticals
- *Working holidays* (alternating recovery and practice)
  - e.g., working on a passion project like writing a book or building a start-up business while taking breaks for decompression and fun, like traveling to a new city or state park, or linking up with friends, then returning to job
- *Free dives* (alternating recovery and exploration)
  - e.g., leaving work to hike the Appalachian Trail and wanting time to deeply reflect, maybe returning to your presabbatical profession, but not necessarily your exact former work—like a nurse leaving a hospital then returning to work in research and teaching instead of with patients
- *Quests* (unfolding from recovery to exploration to practice)
  - e.g., taking extended time to heal as a last resort because it doesn't feel possible or wise to keep going, but rarely going back to the old job; like an executive at a finance company leaving to open a yoga retreat center

When it comes to taking breaks, what have you already tried? What was it like for you? If you have never taken a big break like a sabbatical, what comes mind when you imagine it?

Imagine that a miracle happened: You wake up and you are allowed to take off as much time as you like without taking a financial hit. Of the three types of sabbaticals listed above, which sounds most appealing to you? Least appealing? Why?

Think about your typical day. Do you already intentionally take any *little* rests or breaks—anywhere from a few moments to around half an hour? How consistently does this happen? If you don't, try planning something simple like a 5-minute break once a day and notice what happens.

Imagine a swimmer taking one big breath and swimming the whole length of a pool—they come up gasping for air at the end. Now, imagine someone swimming the breaststroke, coming up for air each stroke along the same route. If your workday is the length of the pool, what are some ways that you could intentionally "come up for air" along the way? (For example, "I can plan meals with colleagues that force a break in my schedule," or "I can set a timer when I'm writing and stand up to shake it off every 40 minutes," or "I can leave something I need in the car so I have to take a quick walk to get it midday.")

ACTIVITY 3C
Sleep Hygiene Checklist

A meta-analysis of almost two hundred studies conducted in more than fifteen countries found that women are more physically and emotionally exhausted than men, accounting for their higher rates of burnout in many sectors, such as media. "An awful lot of middle-aged women are furious and overwhelmed," wrote Ada Calhoun [2016]. . . . What we don't talk about enough is how the deck is stacked against their feeling any other way.

—SORAYA CHEMALY

Goal
To get familiar with evidence-based habits that can contribute to improved sleep, to assess your current rituals and routines, and if needed, to select some small changes that feel worth trying and make a plan.

Instructions
Read through writer Eric Suni and sleep medicine physician David Rosen's sleep hygiene tips below (Rosen & Suni, 2024).

- ❏ Have a fixed wake-up time
- ❏ Prioritize sleep

- ❏ Make gradual adjustments
- ❏ Limit naps to early afternoon and keep them short
- ❏ Try to keep your routine consistent each night
- ❏ Budget 30 minutes for winding down before bed
- ❏ Keep lights dim and avoid bright light before bed
- ❏ Unplug from electronics (e.g., cell phones, tablets, laptops) 30–60 minutes before bed
- ❏ Instead of making falling asleep the goal, make relaxation the goal
- ❏ Avoid tossing and turning: if you haven't fallen asleep after 20 minutes, get up and do something boring or relaxing in low light, then try again
- ❏ Get exposure to daylight, especially sunlight
- ❏ Be physically active (as ability permits)
- ❏ Reduce alcohol consumption
- ❏ Cut down on caffeine in the afternoon and evening
- ❏ Avoid late dining, especially heavy meals
- ❏ Restrict in-bed activity only to sleep and sex
- ❏ Set the house at a cool temperature (around 65 degrees Fahrenheit)
- ❏ Block out light with a mask or blackout curtains and drown out noise
- ❏ Try adding in calming scents (e.g., lavender) to your environment/routine

Looking at the above list, which habits are you already incorporating successfully? Of the items listed, which have historically helped you the most? The least? Any you haven't tried?

What blocks or barriers might come up in your typical week that could get in the way of sleep hygiene? What's the hardest part right now about getting rest?

How do you feel after thinking about your sleep habits? What might you need when you feel this way? (For example, *I feel totally hopeless and more exhausted. I think I need to take a break from this chapter for a minute and go outside for a bit.*)

If you were going to intentionally focus on one or two of these habits, which would be the easiest to begin working on? Do you need to recruit anyone for help or support here?

Relational Activity Add-On: Ask your partner and/or family members to look at the checklist with you. See if you can brainstorm some ideas together that could help with your habits.

ACTIVITY 3D
Discernment—When to Walk Away

> Sometimes you can tell what something is by what it isn't.
> —KENNETH COPELAND

Goal
To begin to consider more deeply what "taking space" means and looks like in your context, and to think through some ways to be able to sense when it is better to step back—even if it's financially tricky—than to continue to try to push forward.

Instructions
Look over the following list of questions you can ask before stepping back from a job or role. Jot down any notes you feel are helpful. Then, create your Cons and Cons list, to begin to move through internal gridlock and to think about old problems in some new ways.

Please note: Parents and caregivers, stepping back will obviously look different for you than it would in a work/training environment, but you can still benefit from this exercise. Stepping back might involve delegating, asking for help, and/or getting childcare—especially if you've been trying to do everything mostly by yourself. You might be in a season where it's extremely difficult or impossible to step back from certain roles (e.g., chestfeeding an infant, or not able to spend much time away). If it feels right, you are invited to skip ahead to the Cons and Cons part of the activity for your situations (e.g., cons of starting daycare 3 days a week vs. cons of staying in the current mode).

- Does your salary/pay reflect your value? Considering how you are compensated, does it feel fair?
- Is your boss an abusive or harmful person? Coworkers? Is the environment generally abusive?
- Is there room to grow in your current position? Have you maxed out on how much you can learn? Are growth opportunities being provided/promised?
- Does the role/job make the most of your unique talents and gifts? Does it help you on your path to a dream, ambition, or goal?
- How long have you been sensing this or feeling this way? Have you done everything you can to try to make things feel better? Have you spoken to your employers about every option?
- Is it possible that you're in the totally wrong position, role, or career for you?
- What do your closest friends think and say about your role or job? Your family? Your therapist?
- Can you afford to quit before you find a new job? If yes, what's stopping you?
- What do you envision next for yourself? If you were to resign or step way back, what would your plan be for what's next? Who could you reach out to for support through this?

Create Your Cons and Cons List

Over the last decade working with couples, rather than the traditional "Pros and Cons" list, I've come to prefer a "Cons and Cons" list. Often it's easy to think of a pro for every con, but this ends up being wildly unhelpful in making decisions. Instead, by listing the cons of choosing one option versus the cons of choosing the other option, you can clearly see the consequences you expect from your choices. You will probably not stumble into a magical solution by doing this—it's to help grease the wheels if you're feeling stuck.

On a sheet of paper, please list the cons of staying in your position—continuing doing the same thing—and the cons of making the change you are considering, such as quitting, leaving, or some form of stepping back. Once you've made your list, please complete the following prompts.

> How was it for you making this list? What sorts of thoughts and feelings are showing up for you looking at the two columns now?
>
> If you suddenly tomorrow when you woke up you were living your ideal/dream scenario, how would it look? What would be different? What wouldn't change?
>
> Think about a time when you had to make a tough decision or choice and you ended up more-or-less pleased and happy with the outcome. What are some of your strengths and qualities that facilitated you figuring it out back then?
>
> Now, think about a time you made a big choice that you ended up really regretting. What was happening when you made this choice? How is this example different from the previous example of a time you felt good about a past choice?
>
> If you're feeling as stuck as you were before thinking through this, what's that like? What's happening in your body? Which parts of you

are feeling the most distressed? (For example, *My impatient part just wants an answer; my perfectionist part is so annoyed.*)

Relational Activity Add-On: If you have a trusted loved-one, friend, or partner who has directly observed you in your burnout, ask them what their hopes and dreams are for you, related to your role. What are they longing for? What would they say the ideal outcome is? The worst case?

EVALUATE AND PLAN TO USE THIS KEY (OR NOT!)

Below are some prompts you can use to evaluate and plan.

How was this third key for you? Any new knowledge or understandings? Any bits or parts you really connected with or liked? Anything you'd like to immediately return to sender?

What I took from this key and the activities was really that ___ (summarize). (For example, "Even if I can't walk away from my stressors for some time, I can begin to feel a little better by intentionally carving out some recurring, as-consistent-as-possible downtime for myself.")

My specific plan for how I'll use this key is ___ (e.g., "I'll look at the next six months in my calendar and plan some small breaks biweekly, and some bigger breaks every two months").

If it feels alright, check in with your body and see if you're needing anything right now. Do you need to stand up and shake it off a bit? Go for a walk? Are you craving a good hug from your favorite person or furry companion? Time for a little snack? I want to invite you attend to your needs.

FINAL THOUGHTS

You covered some serious ground in this chapter, from brain health to breaks, sleep and rest, and even making those tough decisions about stepping back or walking away all together. How's your energy level feeling? Are you tired of hearing about how much you need to rest when there's just not much time available to you right now? One thing I'd like to echo here is that "little" things are *not* little. Lying still for an hour in a quiet, relaxing space counts for something if you feel like you can't sleep. Closing yourself in your pantry while you eat a sweet treat and breathe out for a moment counts. Asking for your colleague to pick you up on their way to save you an hour bike ride counts.

Now, if there aren't major barriers to getting enough sleep for you but you are, say, scrolling your phone or something before bed because it's time to yourself without someone needing your care or help, I invite you to experiment with meeting your need for downtime in some different ways. Sleep and downtime are both important, but if you are struggling especially with more physical symptoms of exhaustion, prioritize rest.

If you are struggling with serious symptoms related to inadequate or disturbed sleep, if it's possible for you, I cannot recommend participating in a sleep study strongly enough. In the past 10 years I've personally referred numerous clients for a medical evaluation who ended up receiving a sleep apnea diagnosis—it's wild how much easier life can get once you get enough oxygen at night! I've also seen a handful of clients get diagnosed with narcolepsy. I'm obviously not a medical doctor, but I especially recommend getting things checked out if partners or family have reported that you snore a lot or there's a family history of apneas or sleep disorders. Even if there's no cure or perfect treatment for your condition, getting appropriate accommodations for school or work can seriously help with burnout management.

In the next chapter you'll learn more about dealing with

stress—and not just reducing or removing stress! A big game changer in stress management is looking not at things to get rid of but at things to intentionally do, to add in, and to cultivate. If you are ready to get really practical and lessen the suffering you are experiencing, you are going to like Key 4.

KEY 4

Do Something With the Stress

> Stress is the trash of modern life. We all generate it, but if you don't dispose of it properly, it will pile up and overtake your life.
>
> —DANZAE PACE

If you've been waiting for the more solution-focused parts of this book, you've fully arrived! This chapter gives you a chance to think about what to do when the rubber meets the road. When I first start working with a client who is burning out, even just the phrase *stress management* can easily elicit a sigh or scoff. What is the first thing that comes to mind as you read that phrase right now? It would not shock me at all if you told me that you have already participated in a number of stress-management-focused workshops or mandatory trainings for work. I would also not be shocked if you told me that you didn't get much out of them. At least, that's what therapy clients report—especially those in health care and education. Through this chapter, you'll learn how your body gears up to deal with stress and some practical, evidence-based things you can tangibly *do* to make sure that you can move through the stress and its accompanying emotions, without getting stuck. Key 4 will help you think about the ever-elusive topic of *balance*.

Therapist Gabor Maté offers one of my favorite definitions for this idea of "balance." He says that *homeostasis* is not, in fact, about perfect balance—it is balance, plus a little extra saved up for a rainy day. Extending this idea, Maté would say that stress is basically when this homeostasis—this balance—feels threatened. Our bodies aren't exactly like bank accounts, but it can be helpful to think of your protections against the effects of stress like deposits. Those who manage their burnout most efficiently are those who persistently, intentionally make little deposits into their account here and there, often on schedule that keeps them consistent. If you aren't being intentional, it can be easy for the account to go into the red—into debt—only you don't get a reminder text from your bank! You will feel better by learning about your own internal bank account. For example, when I know that I'm "in the black"—when I've put in lots of deposits that my body, brain, mind, and relationships need to thrive—I can "spend" more, for example, lend a hand to a friend going through a hard time, even if I'm also stressed out.

The problem with many of the best known stress-management techniques is that they fail to adequately account for a few key features of human neurobiology and psychology:

> How the primitive, unconscious parts of your body rapidly, automatically react to stress (even more so if you're a trauma survivor)
>
> How deeply wired you are to thrive when you are feeling connected and not isolated
>
> How much our engagement in the world and thriving stems from having purpose and making meaning in life

If you don't have any major disorders or disabilities, when your body encounters a stressor, it automatically gives you the ingredients you need to survive: adrenaline, epinephrine, cortisol, and so forth. Have your hands ever gotten shaky when you were nervous about something? Racing heart? Sweaty palms? If yes, you've already noticed the effects of these threat-response ingredients. The trouble is that, if you can't put the ingredients to use—for example, if you can't take your boss into a boxing ring, or sprint away from the dentist—you end up, basically, with an overflowing cup: you end up stuck. And being stuck can even show up as full-on anxiety, depression and suicidal ideation, and/or panic. Key 4 offers a variety of ways to approach stress more practically and realistically, even if the stress level simply will not change much any time soon.

THEORY AND BACKGROUND

Have you heard of the stress-response cycle? This is how your body gears up to deal with perceived threats and danger and then comes back down to your normal baseline when the stressor has passed. Your body basically has a gas pedal and a brake pedal for navigating this. The gas pedal is your *sympathetic nervous system*—it helps get us going when we need to run or fight in the face of a perceived threat. Your gas pedal might give you shaky hands, pounding chest, difficulty thinking, agitation, and so on. Cortisol, adrenaline, norepinephrine—these are materials your body gives you to gear up. And another interesting thing it does to save energy is to suppress your immune system. Once the threat has passed, your body hits the brakes—this is your *parasympathetic nervous system*; your body gives you GABA, acetylcholine, and other materials to chill back out.

What happens if your body gives you materials to gear up to fight off a threat, but it is not appropriate for you to run away or begin an attack? One thing we have to remember about human bodies is that our tissues can't tell the difference between, say, a shark and an angry boss. If you were swimming and saw a shark, your body would give you what you need to attempt an escape (or fight, if you're trapped). Let's say you swim for your life and you make it safely to shore—you see the dorsal fin turn and fade out into the distance and then you collapse in the arms of the lifeguard. In this example, you used up the materials your body gave you—you swam for your life, maybe even more powerfully than ever before, because of all the stress hormones, and you escaped. You just "completed" the stress-response cycle. In a different example, fishermen in a boat nearby noticed your distress and pulled you out of the water—in this case, your body hasn't used the materials pumped out to manage the threat, so you have an "incomplete" stress-response cycle. There are ways to help finish the stress cycle—maybe you run a few hundred yards back to your family to tell that what you survived. In fact, research has shown there are seven ways to "complete" the cycle (Nagoski & Nagoski, 2019), as you will explore in Activity 4A.

Remember how I said that the primitive parts of our bodies that help us survive have a hard time telling the difference between threats? You might notice yourself get just as shaky when you see that dorsal fin as when a salty boss calls you into the office to reprimand you. Your body still gets you ready to run or fight, but because you don't want to lose your job, you just stay still and listen, and then go straight back to work. To use up the stress-response materials hanging out in your body, you would need to *do* something after interacting with your boss. Imagine every time your boss fusses and you feel stressed out, a little liquid is added to a cup—by the end of the day, is it overflowing? By the end of the week? There are proven ways to keep this spillover from happening. Attending to this spillover is an essential part of stopping burnout.

One additional piece that I want to tie in, if you're cohabitating with someone and raising kids: the *mental load*, the cognitive, emotional, and physical labor needed to run a household. When I'm working with a couple, it's painfully easy to tell who is managing the bulk of the mental load—who spends more energy/time anticipating needs, organizing, planning, and, frankly, getting things done. If there are two of you raising kids, can both of you tell me the height and weight of all your kids? Who the doctor and dentist are? Where everyone goes on Thursday after school? Are there AA batteries at home and where? Who picks up birthday gifts on the way to friends' birthday parties? If there is a lack of balance in this domain, you can expect relational disconnection and even distress, in addition to burnout. Yet things don't have to feel *exactly* 50/50 for there to be a sense of fairness. The only way you can ensure that things feel fair in your relationship is to make time to check in together.

More often than not, for a cis man and woman in a heterosexual relationship with children, it's the woman who's feeling overwhelmed and unfairly managing too much of the mental load. This is especially true for "care tasks"—these are required consistently and never-endingly, such as cleaning, caring for kids' daily needs, and cooking. If you are feeling burnt out primarily because you don't have enough help and support at home and you are struggling to bring this up or explain this to your partner, a relationship counselor can be a great resource! Even if you are in a season when things can't change much, or it's as fair as you can manage it for the time being, making sure things are named and acknowledged directly and out loud can increase emotional attunement and decrease stress. This will make more sense once you've completed Activity 4B, Name It To Tame It.

RESEARCH-BASED IMPACTS OF CARRYING THE MENTAL LOAD

- Angry outbursts
- Distraction from paid work or leisure activities
- Exhaustion
- Feelings of emptiness
- Feeling overwhelmed
- Greater bedtime worries or stress
- Having little time for oneself
- Increased anxiety
- Increased feelings of depression
- Lower satisfaction with one's partner

- Poor sleep quality
- Relationship conflict

Source: Ciciolla and Luthar (2019)

DISCOVERING THE KEY

Admittedly, I began to discover this key only after I had completed graduate school, burnt out, moved to New York City briefly, and then back to Texas. Where I live, to get licensed as a counselor, you need to complete at least two internships: one shorter pre-grad internship while you're still in school, and a second 3,000 hour post-grad internship working under a supervisor after you finish grad school. However, when I finished grad school, instead of looking for a practice to join, I moved to Brooklyn, without any explicit plans of continuing to pursue a career in mental health. I was exhausted, listless, beyond cynical, covered in eczema, and struggling with headaches and fatigue. All of this was compounded with guilt—I had just spent three years and an incredible amount of effort getting my master's degree, and my family had invested so much in me, emotionally and financially. And there I was, throwing my hands up. I took the first job I was offered and became a personal assistant to a blind jazz pianist and performer. Not that it wasn't a cool gig, but it didn't call for the full range of skills or specialization I had painstakingly acquired over the previous three years of grad school and four years of undergrad.

When I think back on this time, I don't wish that it never happened. I wouldn't be anywhere near as interesting without these few years. And learning what you're *not* is a useful way to sort out what you are meant to be. But, I regret not knowing what to do with the stress in my body, mind, and relationships. When you're a therapist (or expert on health of any sort, really), the irony can feel painful at times—there I was, trained to support others to navigate distress, absolutely drowning in my own life. When I had settled back in Austin after my misadventures in Brooklyn, about halfway through my 3,000 hour internship, the daily felt-sense of beating my head against the wall—overworked and underpaid—had me on the brink of walking away from the field for a second time. But I *loved* the work and adored the clients I was serving. It felt like a curse: The thing I happened to be best at felt like it was going to be the end of me. But I knew that once I was fully licensed, I could set my own schedule and earn more—things would get better, it was just not clear when.

A simple yet profound concept I learned from Emily Nagoski and Amelia Nagoski's 2019 book *Burnout* is this: You need to actively, consistently—habitually and ritually—*do* things to prevent burnout, and you can do them more efficiently if you understand more about the human body and how the brain works. Instead of waiting for the occasional weekend retreat or burnout workshop, I started focusing on small things every day. Even today, I see myself a bit like a cup: I get filled up each day, and if I do not intentionally empty out, the spillover eventually floods the room and I end up under water, burnt out. The upcoming activities will help you learn more about your body and brain and why you need more than traditional stress management techniques to avoid and recover from burnout.

ACTIVITY 4A
Seven Ways to Complete the Stress-Response Cycle

> No matter how much falls on us, we keep plowing ahead. That's the only way to keep the roads clear.
>
> —GREG KINCAID

Goal

To learn multiple different ways to complete the stress-response cycle and to practically think through ways to implement and make changes in your day-to-day life.

Instructions

Please look through the following list of seven evidence-based ways to complete the stress-response cycle. Then, answer the subsequent prompt questions.

1. Physical activity (e.g., joyful movement or exercise)
2. Positive social interaction (e.g., hanging with your trusted best friend)
3. Intentional breathing (e.g., extended out-breath breathing)
4. Laughter
5. Affection (e.g., with partner, pet, or higher power)
6. Crying
7. Creative expression (e.g., music, art, writing)

Of these seven techniques, which do you already do on a daily/weekly basis? Which happen less frequently?

If you wanted to plan to add something into your routine on a daily basis—remembering that focusing on small things every day can be more helpful than trying for a giant dose every few weeks or months—which seem(s) the easiest and most practical for your current life?

Consider the sorts of adaptations you'd need to make if you wanted to try this throughout your day, for instance, if you're at work when you have coworkers around you, or if you're supporting children, elderly, or disabled people who may need a higher level of care/attention. What are relatively simple/small things you can do and still attend to your responsibilities? (For example, if my boss yells at me, I can go to the bathroom and privately do some jumping jacks to complete the stress cycle; if the baby wouldn't stop crying after lying down, for a few minutes after they settle, I can breathe in for 4 seconds, hold the breath for 7 seconds, and then exhale for 8 seconds.)

What kinds of barriers or blocks might get in the way of you doing this? What could you do to help in spite of these? (For example, I'm not permitted to take as many breaks at work as I need to complete cycles—Can I advocate for myself by asking for this at work?) Can you make time at the end of the day or on the way home from work instead? Do you need childcare to be able to do this?

Does this exercise bring up any feelings of frustration or hopelessness? Any other feelings or memories? What might you need to comfortably move through these feelings in the moment?

Please note: One activity that a lot of clients like which you can feel invited to try if it appeals, is to make a "menu" of options of ways to complete the cycle, which you can refer to at a glance to remind you. You could write out a list and put it on the fridge, or write one sticky note for each possible thing to try and put those on a whiteboard. When you're overwhelmed and stressed out, it can be hard to remember everything that helps. And if you're like me and have some executive function stuff going on because of ADHD or neurodivergence, if you don't *see* it, it may as well not exist. If you have kids, this is also a great activity to teach about emotions and bodies, so feel invited to do it together as a family.

Relational Activity Add-On: Ask your partner, friend, loved one, or mentor if they'd like to do something with you to complete the stress cycle. What could you do together that wouldn't take too much effort or time, and wouldn't be an inappropriate distraction to coworkers or family?

ACTIVITY 4B
Name It to Tame It

> When you experience significant internal tension and anxiety, you can reduce stress by up to 50% by simply noticing and naming your state.
>
> —DAVID ROCK

Goal

To get familiar with interpersonal neurobiologist Dan Siegel's technique "Name it to tame it" (Siegel, 2013) to downregulate—calm—the threat detection centers in your brain and help decrease distress. This can be used both individually and in relationships and families.

Side quest for parents: Search "Dan Siegel hand-brain model video," which helps kids as young as 5 begin to understand how their brain works and impacts changes in emotions.

Instructions

Please read Siegel's (2023) description below and the example that follows. Then, complete the subsequent prompts to help you think through how you might use this in a practical way in your own unique context.

> In the brain, naming an emotion can help calm it. Here is where finding words to label an internal experience becomes really helpful. We can call this "Name it to tame it." And sometimes these [automatic] states can go beyond being unpleasant and confusing—they can even make life feel terrifying. If that is going on, talk about it. Sharing your experience with others can often make even terrifying moments understood and not traumatizing.

For example, imagine you've arrived home from work—which already felt like one of the longest shifts in recorded history—and you are exhausted and overstimulated. Today, you helped everyone and their dog, just not really yourself. When you walk in the door at home, your toddler is having a meltdown on the floor, screaming bloody murder. Your partner gives you the "S.O.S." look.

Even if you do need to lend a hand in the moment, you can quite literally calm your body in this moment of stress just by naming it, something like, "I'm feeling overwhelmed." If your partner then says, with a supportive tone, "You're overwhelmed—was it a long shift?", that's even better, because now the primitive parts of your body sense, "I'm not alone here."

Other Examples of Naming Your Internal Experiences

- Sadness. I'm sad.
- I'm feeling stressed about work.
- My face and ears feel hot, I'm so angry right now.
- The thought of ____ (concern/worry; e.g., not having a break this weekend) has me feeling really anxious right now.
- I'm feeling a bit defensive right now. The story I'm telling myself is it's not okay to make mistakes and that what I do right won't be noticed.
- When I hear you say ____ (repeat the exact words they used), I notice that I feel ____ (emotions/feelings or sensations; e.g., lonely, stressed, sad, my heart start to race, my stomach drop).

Please note: Depending on the situation/context, you can name things in many different ways:

- Aloud to yourself
- Internally to yourself

- Written out journaling style
- Aloud to someone else (e.g., partner, therapist, therapy group)
- Internally to someone else (e.g., prayer, connection with ancestors, loving-kindness meditation)

In your life presently, if you wanted to practice naming things aloud, who might be a safe person/people to try this with? Who might *not* be a good candidate?

If sharing this way is not something you've really done before, what might you say to recruit someone you trust? (For example, "I've read that just saying out loud how I feel might help with my stress. Would it be okay if sometimes I let you know that I just need someone to listen and not give advice?")

How was talking about feelings modeled in your environment growing up? Are there any parts of you that feel like this is a bad idea or like it would not be helpful to name things?

Feel invited to design your own experiment! Perhaps you let your partner know that you're going to "name it to tame it" when you come in the door at the end of the day. Notice what it feels like before *and* after you put words to your state. Does it work better if you write it in a journal? If you say it out loud? If you name it to a friend? Everyone is different, so give yourself some grace and permission to try multiple approaches.

ACTIVITY 4C
Joyful Movement and Exercise

> Peace is joy at rest, and joy is peace on its feet.
>
> —REVEREND VERONICA GOINES

Goal

To assess your current physical activity level relative to your abilities and to think through some ways to keep your body moving while minimizing/removing body negativity.

Instructions

Read through the following brief definition of joyful movement, some examples from me, and then respond to the prompts that follow, jotting down any notes that feel helpful.

Joyful movement: movement that is fun and enjoyable, not punishing or for the sole purpose of making/keeping your body smaller. (Tribole & Resch, 2017)

Potential sources of joyful movement include:

- Gardening
- Gentle stretching
- Playing with kids
- Taking a pet for a walk
- Swimming or gently moving in water
- Activities adapted for disabled people, like wheelchair basketball or water skiing
- Trying a trampoline park
- Dance or gently moving part of your body to music
- Horseback riding
- Dodgeball
- Yoga
- Intimate activities or sex
- Hiking

- Tai Chi
- Cycling or social biking
- Paddleboarding

Please note: Be aware that emotional and mental wellness can be negatively impacted if movement is motivated solely by self-critical thoughts, fear, or punishment. Workouts that have an exclusively brutal, self-punishing feel confuse the primitive parts of your body into thinking you're not safe. *Joyful* movement, in contrast, gives your body signals of *safety*.

Do you already have an intentional routine including physical movement or exercise? How consistent is it?

What do you notice about your thoughts about yourself when you're about to move, exercise, or work out? While you're active? After you've finished?

What kinds of physical activities/movement have tended to make you feel joyful, during and after? If it's been a while, think about what you liked to do as a kid or in school (e.g., walking the dog, playing outside, taking a hike, biking to work).

If you don't already have a routine that includes a little joyful movement at least once a week, what is one way you could add in half an hour, even 10 minutes, without significantly disrupting your schedule?

If you frequently think, "I have no free time!" or feel like, "When am I supposed to do *more* things?!", please know that *small* things *daily* often have the biggest impact. Where are there some small moments in your day-to-day when you could move your body in a way that feels joyful (or distinctly not awful)? *Hint:* Clients often report that transitions, such as going from work to home, provide solid opportunities for a little focus on joyful movement (e.g., getting in/out of bed, walking to the car, going to the grocery store).

ACTIVITY 4D
Coming Up for Air

> Caring for myself is not self-indulgence. It's self-preservation.
>
> —AUDRE LORDE

Goal
To get familiar with some ways to feel refreshed and reinvigorated and to come up with some ideas for how to use your precious free time in ways that are actually renewing.

Instructions
Read through the brief summary of research findings from the 2021 study by Clément Ginoux, Sandrine Isoard-Gautheur, and Philippe Sarrazin on activities for renewal from burnout, and then complete the prompts that follow.

Ginoux et al. (2021) found five characteristics of activities that most impact renewal and recovery from burnout:

1. *Detachment* (e.g., not doing work-related things on the weekend, reading things unrelated to work, practicing redirection/distraction when thoughts of work arise)
2. *Relaxation* (e.g., solo, with your partner/family, or with a group of friends)
3. *Mastery* (e.g., doing things in your free time that allow you to notice your talents and appreciate your skills)

4. *Control* (e.g., working to influence groups that contribute to your sense of meaning or identity, or doing activities where you have a felt sense of control)
5. *Relatedness* (e.g., connecting and collaborating with others, spending time with loved ones)

When you think about your free time, which of these characteristics already describe the activities you engage in? How consistently do you have these experiences month to month?

If you haven't been doing much with the little free time you have, which characteristic(s) might be the easiest to increase in or add to your present life? Which might be more challenging?

If you have very little free time and you wanted to curate an activity that includes two or more of the above characteristics, what might be some possibilities? What would absolutely *not* work?

If you draw a Venn diagram in your mind of your social connections—those associated with work and those outside of work—how much overlap is there?

If most of your social interactions involve people from work, how much time do you spend talking/thinking about work together *outside* of work? You need to spend time together that has absolutely nothing to do with work. How might you let a colleague know you're working at this? Do you have any friends outside of work you haven't seen in a while who might be fun to reconnect with? It can be worth checking out some meetups or local community organizations and events, if you are at this point thinking, *but . . . I have no friends*. Positive social connection completes the stress cycle, as you know, and we're healthier, medically and emotionally, when we sense that someone has our back when things get tough.

Relational Activity Add-On: If you work with your partner or loved one and it's hard for you to spend time together without bringing up work, brainstorm one thing you could try together at least 30–60 minutes each week to disconnect from work. If you try it and like it, how can you carve out time for it regularly?

EVALUATE AND PLAN TO USE THIS KEY (OR NOT!)

Below are some prompts you can use to evaluate and plan.

> How was this fourth key for you? Any new knowledge or understandings? Any bits or parts you really connected with or liked? Anything you'd like to immediately return to sender?
>
> What I took from this key and the activities was really that ____ (summarize). (For example, "If I intentionally work to complete the stress-response cycle more weeks than not—especially if I'm including joyful movement!—I have a better shot at keeping regulated.")
>
> My specific plan for how I'll use this key is ____ (e.g., "I'll start by doing one hour of joyful movement each week for the next 6 weeks to see how it impacts me").

Checking in with yourself, is there anything you need after completing the activities in this chapter? Because of the intense body negativity and shaming in our culture, I want to note that it's normal if talking about physical activity stirs up a mix of emotions or self-criticism for you. If you're noticing being a little hard on yourself, what is one way that you could show yourself some kindness before you continue reading?

FINAL THOUGHTS

Let's have another look at the quote by Danzae Pace at the start of this chapter: "Stress is the trash of modern life. We all generate it, but if you don't dispose of it properly, it will pile up and overtake your life." Now you have a sense of what "taking out the trash" looks like, and you know a few practical things you can do to keep the trash from piling up. It's an excellent metaphor! I lived in a neighborhood once where recycling only came every 2 weeks, so if I forgot to take it to the curb once, a 4-week backlog would build up. The image comes to mind of my recycling bin in the driveway overflowing, the recycling bin in the kitchen overflowing, and a couple of bags stacked in the garage waiting 2 weeks to go to the curb. When I've been in the worst parts of my own burnout, I have felt like this: overflowing, always behind, and never really able to actually, really get on top of things, much less ahead of them!

So, to stick with this metaphor, we're best served when we're (a) consistently picking up items of trash from around the house and bagging it up, and (b) periodically putting all of the bags in a bin and taking it to the curb. *More weeks than not* and *more days than not* are phrases I love in this context, especially if you're someone with an assertive inner perfectionist. So my invitation to you is not to set a specific goal for every single time, every single day, but to be able to say, "More days than not in a month, I intentionally do things to complete stress-response cycles." And perhaps you can add, when the time is right, "More months than not, I intentionally do something more intensive than usual to keep a little saved for a rainy day."

Key 4 is most applicable to people experiencing a lot of stress—for surviving day to day without exploding or stagnating. There's a difference between managing and healing. If you've primarily got to manage right now, you now have some practical ideas that will help. The next chapter touches more on what to do if you're in a position/role where daily stressors are likely to persist, at least for a time. Key

5 will provide more opportunities for you to take your understanding beyond stress management. Effectively dealing with burnout requires concurrent focus on what you're releasing, and what you're adding in—you will feel more successful if you focus not just on stopping unpleasant sensations but also on actively increasing your felt sense of safety, pleasure, and connection.

KEY 5

Figure Out What Keeps Your Fire Going

A good half of the art of living is resilience.

—ALAIN DE BOTTON

Hope is not optimism, which expects things to turn out well, but something rooted in the conviction that there is good worth working for.

—SEAMUS HEANEY

Keeping yourself from burning out isn't just about reducing or removing stress from your life. It's also about what you intentionally *add in*—what and who you connect with. There will be times when you have no other choice but to adapt to a stressor, for example, if you are in a training program that lasts a few years before you're fully licensed, or you are getting out of debt and the salary you have can get you there in a couple years. Sometimes there's a nightmare person built in at your dream job. Parenting and caregiving obviously also call for this type of longer form adaptation. To really flourish—to feel connected with yourself and the world around you—you have to make sure to both remove/reduce some of the bad and intentionally add in the good. You can't just, for instance, run five miles every day to deal with the stress and expect to feel your best. A lot of men I work with as clients stop saying, "The gym is my therapy," because they recognize the gym is just a part of what helps (even if it's a big part).

Keep that concept on the front burner: It's not just about a lack of stress, removing stress—it's about the presence of a felt sense of *safety, pleasure, and joy*, of connection and emotional balance. In her book *Polyvagal Theory in Therapy: Engaging the Rhythm of Regulation* (2018), therapist Deb Dana says the job of your autonomic nervous system is "to ensure we survive in moments of danger and thrive in times of safety. Survival requires threat detection and the activation of a survival response. Thriving demands the opposite—the inhibition of survival response so that social engagement can happen. Without the capacity for activation, inhibition, and flexibility of response, we suffer." This key is about trying for thriving, not just scraping by.

Another big part of this key has to do with building flexibility—not in the gymnastics sense but in terms of being able to shift from one state to another, to move intentionally into "rest and digest" mode, or to change from sympathetic "fight–flight" activation to being in social engagement mode. A healthy goal here isn't to stay in one mode or another all the time—it's being able to (a) know what gear your body is in, and (b) shift gears if you want or need to. Being able to shift and change the state of your nervous system—especially the automatic parts—not only helps you feel better but also strengthens your ability to navigate conflict and crises while being compassionate to those around you. If you have ever gotten feedback that you are mean or bark orders when you're overwhelmed or dealing with a crisis, this chapter will give you some ways you can improve your interpersonal effectiveness—not be a jerk—to your coworkers and colleagues and to the people you love who see you on a daily basis.

This key will help you learn to better navigate nervous system states, to appreciate the difference between *triggers* and *glimmers*, and to make concrete plans not just to reduce triggers but to increase glimmers. You'll also have the opportunity to try some of the tips and techniques that clients I serve report to be most impactful. You'll learn some ways to navigate blocks and barriers on your way to healing, such as *toxic positivity* and *spiritual bypassing*—basically, what you can do instead of being told to "find the gift" in suffering, or to focus on the "silver lining," to the point that reality is grossly downplayed if not completely ignored.

THEORY AND BACKGROUND

Let's start with some background on resilience and toxic positivity. Whenever I talk to people about what keeps them going through tough times, hope (and faith, if you're spiritual) and resilience are usually the top two responses. Chan Hellman, psychologist and founding director of the Hope Research Center at the University of Oklahoma, said, "We often use the word 'hope' in place of wishing, like you hope it rains today or hope someone's well. But wishing is passive toward a goal, and hope is about taking action toward it" (2024, p. 88). Hope is something that you can actively cultivate! The key is that it takes *action*. In the first activity below, you'll learn a simple way to begin to cultivate hope in your own life.

In her book *Option B: Facing Adversity, Building Resilience, and Finding Joy*, Sheryl Sandberg (2017) describes four core beliefs that you can foster in children to build resilience: (1) they have some control over their lives, (2) they can learn from failure, (3) they matter as human beings, and (4) they have real strengths to rely on, grow, and share. These same four factors, unsurprisingly, ring true for those I've known and served struggling with burnout. If you are in a leadership role wanting to prevent turnover and cultivate a healthy work environment, it is also incredibly smart to consider these themes as you build professional relationships with employees. When I hear people think about resilience, I notice that the focus often gets drawn to traits more traditionally considered to be masculine, such as strength, power, and fortitude. Resilience also has a lot to do with self-awareness, emotional regulation, and attunement. Clients who are nurses, medical students, therapy grad students, and teachers are the first ones who come to mind when I think about this warmer side of resilience—to continue to be kind and compassionate when you are exhausted takes awareness and intention.

Deb Dana (2018) says, "Compassion is only possible when we're in a ventral vagal state." It's okay if you're thinking, *What in the world is a ventral vagal state?* or, *How do I get to that state?* I'm going to give you the briefest of introductions to Stephen Porges's *Polyvagal Theory* (2011), and I'll use Dana's polyvagal ladder from *Polyvagal Theory In Therapy* (2018) to help make it more digestible. Have a look at the polyvagal ladder image in Figure 5.1 (you can also call it the *autonomic ladder*).

For some clients, it helps to imagine the ladder as a traffic light: red (dorsal), yellow (sympathetic), and green (ventral). Your aim is to begin to increase your awareness of the state your nervous system is in—by *state* I mean like a gear that you can shift to go into a different mode. The tricky thing is, our bodies are so specialized for certain kinds of survival that they'll shift gears without our conscious awareness, and even without our consent sometimes—especially if you've survived a trauma. For the purposes of this chapter, you mainly need to know that you can be at the top of the ladder, or the bottom, or anywhere in between. At the top of the ladder, or ventral vagal, you'll feel like yourself, comfy and able to socially engage and connect. In the middle, or sympathetic/fight-flight, you'll notice more feelings of agitation or flightiness. Finally, at the bottom of the ladder, or dorsal vagal, you may feel numb, frozen, or struggle to think or speak. And being able to recognize where you are lets you give yourself what you need (or request support) to shift in the direction you want. Increasing awareness and flexibility here helps loads of clients, especially those trying to do incredibly difficult work while keeping their heart and soul intact and available to those they serve when needed.

You can feel empowered to know that it is possible to intentionally

FIGURE OUT WHAT KEEPS YOUR FIRE GOING 103

FIGURE 5.1
Polyvagal Ladder

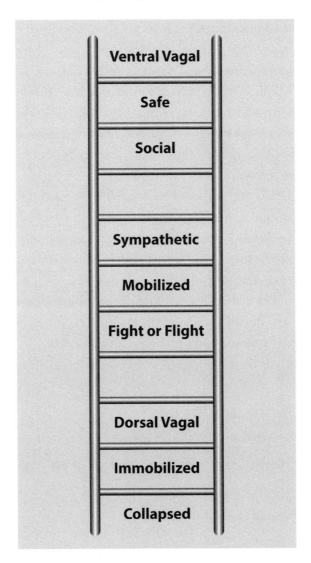

From THE POLYVAGAL THEORY IN THERAPY: ENGAGING THE RHYTHM OF REGULATION by Deb Dana. Copyright © 2018 by Deb Dana. Used by permission of W. W. Norton & Company, Inc.

give your body cues that it is safe to be "in the green"—in the ventral state. A lot of what you're learning in this book is specifically tailored to help you spend more time in this nervous system state, where you're open and receptive to connection and collaboration with others. When in doubt, research shows that, if you want to help let your body know that you are safe, try things you see kids doing—playing, laughing, singing and dancing, sitting in the grass with your shoes off. The unconscious parts of your wiring don't listen to words—especially when you're dealing with lots of stress—you have to *show* your body that everything is okay. You need to *do* joy. This chapter offers plenty of chances to think more practically about this and to apply it to your own life.

Is anyone already rolling their eyes with the onslaught of words like *hope*, *joy*, and *resilience*? If I was reading this when I was burnt toast back in 2013, I probably would have had a similar response. That's because I was so used to these words accompanying what psychologist Jaime Zuckerman calls *toxic positivity*, the excessive promotion of positive thinking without taking someone's situation or experience into consideration (Sawhney, 2020, p. 88). Some common toxic positivity phrases you're probably familiar with:

- Good vibes only!
- Everything happens for a reason.
- I did it—you can too!
- There's a silver lining to everything—look on the bright side!
- Just focus on the positive.
- Things could always be worse!

These phrases and those like them can be generally demoralizing. And, if you think back to our foundation of social justice and equity, how are some of these phrases possibly problematic?

It's not uncommon to see wealthy, white influencers on social media talking about how they "manifested" the good things in their life without acknowledging any of their (frequently numerous) privileges.

You may have also heard the phrase *spiritual bypassing*. It's technically a type of toxic positivity, but it was described before that language was originally used. Therapist John Welwood coined the term to represent "using spiritual ideas and practices to sidestep personal, emotional 'unfinished business,' to shore up a shaky sense of self, or to belittle basic needs, feelings, and developmental tasks." If you are on social media, you have already noticed spiritual bypassing: "Anything you want—you just have to manifest it!" "Well you know, the Lord gives his toughest battles to his strongest soldiers." "This is all part of God's plan." "Just give it to God." You are not a bad person if you've said these sorts of things. Your family isn't bad if it cultivates ideas like this.

It's really about the both/and: You could encourage someone you love who believes in God to seek relief in that resource without asking them to deny or suppress their reality. For example, "You're having such a hard time right now. Things are really unfair and you're suffering. I know you said you like to come to prayer group with me sometimes—would you like to join this Sunday? No pressure!"

So what's the opposite of all this toxic positivity? In her book *Toxic Positivity: Keeping It Real in a World Obsessed With Being Happy*, therapist Whitney Goodman (2022) differentiates helpful from toxic positivity. Helpful positivity has these qualities:

- Recognizes the value of seeing the good and allows people to arrive at their own beneficial conclusions and to take their time getting there.

- Recognizes that humans have a variety of emotions, some more challenging than others, and allows people to see the good and bad sides of a situation.
- Has an understanding that not all situations have a silver lining and we will still experience joy.
- Encourages emotional expression from others (with boundaries) and from within ourselves, knowing that for some to experience happiness they often have to process and move through the pain.
- Looks out for and recognizes the highs and lows of a situation.

Willingness to experience the wide range of emotions humans feel without loads of self-judgment or repression is foundational for your ability to be forward-looking and to balance being realistic and *authentically* hopeful about the future. If you've internalized some toxic positivity, you'll have some space to think more about that roadblock in the upcoming activities. And if you are surrounded by people committed to embodying toxic positivity, you'll get a chance to think through some kind ways to, frankly, return that nonsense to sender.

DISCOVERING THE KEY

Before I even realized that intentionally looking forward and healthy positivity help individuals feel uplifted, I was guiding partners in struggling relationships to do this together. I recommend that couples do something together, one-on-one, every week. Finances make it look different for everyone, but I also recommend something like a long weekend or bigger date experience every 2–3 months and one thing together that feels extra special once or twice a year. When partners focus on planning these things together, it's impossible not to notice the energetic lift that tends to happen in their relationship. And you don't have to magically stop all the bad things from happening in life, the obstacles, the stress, the setbacks. You just need to try to *add in* times when you can feel neutral to positive and to plan them in advance so that you can experience healthy, joyful feelings of anticipation instead of the day-to-day dread.

What initially surprised me, and clients I serve, when I first started focusing on this with relationships was that the selected experience or activity planned for the future did not have to be elaborate or expensive to decrease hopelessness, apathy, and distress. The key is not the promise of some lavish vacation or over-the-top, curated experience—it's the promise of intentional time together. Knowing that you have set time aside to do something distinctly not awful is energy giving—it forces a perspective shift. When you are burning out, it is easy to forget that the experience is like a tunnel, not a cave. If you have a very long way to go, the light at the end of the tunnel can feel too far off—it can look too dark. Making positive plans, however small, on the other hand, punctuates your tunnel with lights every so often, lighting and lightening your way.

Over the last few years I've really been specializing with individuals burning out, and I've noticed that this same principle applies to individuals as well. The key is essentially doing whatever we can to remind ourselves that the tunnel is *not* a cave, punctuating our path with light so our eyes are drawn upward and forward, not down into the darkness immediately in front of us. To be clear, I am in no way suggesting you ignore heavy or difficult things life throws at you. This isn't about finding a "silver lining" or merely reframing your suffering—it's about giving our bodies and minds moments without the feeling of stress or stuckness. You can hold these ideas in your mind while also reminding yourself that feeling relief and happiness is an ongoing process and not a destination.

ACTIVITY 5A
Something to Look Forward To

> Without leaps of imagination or dreaming, we lose the excitement of possibilities. Dreaming, after all is a form of planning.
>
> —GLORIA STEINEM

Goal

To evaluate how much you already build things into the fabric of your day-to-day and month-to-month life that you can use to generate energy and enthusiasm by looking forward to, and to think through some ways to consistently continue to orient toward the future in a way that feels good.

Instructions

Please complete the following prompts.

> On a day-to-day basis, are there any *little* things you notice getting excited about, such as getting lunch, talking with your best friend, taking a shower, going for a walk, or having coffee or sweet treat? How about month to month?
>
> In the first half of the year, on average, how many times would you say you get really excited about an upcoming event, activity, trip, or experience? And the second half of the year?
>
> How do you feel about the idea of treating yourself? What did you learn in your early life about what it means to *indulge*?
>
> What were you encouraged to focus on, related to the future? Does your cultural or religious upbringing play into this? How?
>
> If you were to pick one simple, practical thing that makes you even a *little* happy, excited, or relieved, that you could intentionally try to do daily, what might that be? Monthly?

Sometimes what you can look forward to is not the presence of something pleasant but the removal of something unpleasant. (For example, "The person I'm caring for will be able to drive themselves in 6 weeks and my life will get a lot easier.") If you are struggling to think of something to look forward to, is there an end to something that sounds even mildly appealing?

Please note: if you use a paper or digital calendar to stay organized, I invite you to make special note of the upcoming thing you're looking forward to, so that you can visually see and be reminded of it. It can also feel nice to cross off the days as you get closer.

ACTIVITY 5B
Dodge Toxic Positivity

> We often find that the harder we try to get rid of emotions and thoughts, the stronger they become.
>
> —RICHARD SCHWARTZ

Goal
To be able to define and recognize toxic positivity and think through some ways to kindly invite those around you to "just not."

Instructions
First let's review the definition of toxic positivity and examples of associated thoughts and phrases. Next, read through the examples of phrases you can use to uninvite toxic positivity, and then complete the prompts that follow.

> *Toxic positivity*: excessive promotion of positive thinking without taking someone's situation or experience into consideration

Examples of Toxic Positivity

- Good vibes only!
- Everything happens for a reason.
- I did it—you can too!
- There's a silver lining to everything—look on the bright side!
- Just focus on the positive.
- Things could always be worse!

Example Phrases That Uninvite Toxic Positivity

- "I can tell that it's really difficult for you to hear about my suffering. I'm sharing because research shows that naming our emotions actually downregulates our nervous system and makes us feel calmer. Would you prefer that I not do this with you?"

- "Hey, can I ask you about something personal? I'm really going through it right now, and I just need someone I can reach out to occasionally to vent. If I call you and let you know that I just need you to listen and not offer advice, do you think you could do that with me for the next 2 weeks? It would really mean the world."

- "Can I share something a bit vulnerable with you? The phrase ____ (insert toxic positivity phrase) can bring up a lot of painful feelings for me because it was used by ____ (insert circumstance) to silence honesty about emotional experiences. It's so easy for me tell you are only trying to help. Would you like to know what helps me most?" (Describe the support you long for.)

- "I'm about to share something that feels really tender, and I'm not looking for solutions or problem-solving—just a compassionate witness so I feel less alone. Would that be alright?"

- "When I hear you say ____ (insert toxic positivity phrase), I feel ____ (insert emotion or feeling, e.g., alone, dismissed, sad, unheard, unimportant), and the story I end up telling myself is not good. Do

you think, moving forward, you could be mindful about when you say that? I really appreciate you taking time to hear me out here."
- "I appreciate your patience with me here—I'm going to have to stop you. This is not helpful to me. I feel even more alone and broken when I hear language like that, and I really don't think you are trying to make me feel alone and broken. Please stop."

You can also set a boundary: (1) Let them know what's not been feeling good (e.g., "Remember how I asked you to refrain from telling me to identify the silver lining when I'm just having a sad moment? I'm noticing that it's been difficult for you to honor this request"). (2) Let them know how you'll remind them when it happens. (For example, "If I hear that language coming up, I'll remind you of our discussion here, but if it keeps on, I'll need to remove myself from the room. I so appreciate you understanding. I love you so much.") (3) If they begin to violate the boundary, give the reminder, but if they aren't able or refuse to honor your request, name what's happening and then take space. For example, "Hey, I so appreciate you remembering our conversation about this silver lining reminder. I'm going to go ahead and ___ (e.g., take my leave, step out, take a break and come back later, go into the other room, step outside). We can try again in the future!"

And you can advocate for loved ones on their behalf if your relationship supports that. Doing this can also models healthy ways of expressing and processing feelings for people with less knowledge about emotions. For instance, if you hear a parent going off on your sibling, you can interrupt with kindness by saying something like, "It sounds like (*name*) is really just looking for some support and understanding—I didn't hear them ask for advice or reassurance that it's in God's hands. (*Name*), I see you—you're really suffering right now and it sucks. Want to get out of here and go ___ (e.g., on a walk around the neighborhood; get your favorite coffee drink; someplace peaceful where we can chill)?"

Please note: Sometimes it's wisest to bite your tongue in the group and then reach out individually later to the person you wish to support and/or the person embodying toxic positivity.

When you look through the above list of possible responses to friends or family members pushing toxic positivity, what comes to mind? What feelings come up?

If you sense that the majority of people in your life don't have the capacity for interpersonal and emotional skills to honor your requests about toxic positivity, what's that like? Is there anyone in your world who seems like they could show up for you like you really need? (*Tip:* If your answer is no, a helping professional like a therapist or social worker might help you feel some relief.)

ACTIVITY 5C
Glimmers and Triggers

> It is the tiny moments of joy, the moments of "okayness" that take us away from being stuck in this challenging world we're in or our own trauma that's sitting unprocessed, and it . . . helps build the capacity to then manage these things in a different way.
>
> —DEB DANA

Goal
To be able to differentiate triggers and glimmers, to take inventory of some of your own, and to plan ways to increase experiences of glimmers in day-to-day life.

Instructions
Read the definitions of triggers *and* glimmers, a term coined by trauma therapist Deb Dana, and then complete the prompts that follow.

Triggers: events/experiences (anything you see, smell, taste, touch, imagine, think, or believe) that overwhelm us and activate—"trigger"—our defensive responses (e.g., fight, flight)

Glimmers: opposite of triggers; "micro-moments of safety, connection, and regulation"; small moments that bring joy and can help when you're feeling immobilized

What are some "little" things, small moments that you already notice bringing joy to your life, even if it's just a teeny bit (e.g., doing something creative, listening to a favorite song, getting coffee with friends)? If you aren't experiencing many glimmers right now, where might be some small openings or opportunities for one or two in your daily routine?

When are some times that you maybe don't feel really positive or negative but more neutral—distinctly not awful, but also not thrilled? Intentionally doing things that are neutral feeling can also count, especially if you're in a really raw season where pleasure is in short supply.

Please note: If you're having a hard time thinking of things that glimmer for you, it can help to ask a friend or partner to share what they notice about you. When do they see you smile or giggle? What do they notice seems to light your fire? When have you seemed the most peaceful or joyful recently, and what were you doing?

ACTIVITY 5D
Reconnect With What Lights You Up

> The most sophisticated people I know—
> inside they are all children.
>
> —JIM HENSON

Goal

To identify and work to intentionally cultivate experiences with ease and joy, in particular, some that look and feel similar to what sparked joy in you in early life.

Instructions

First, please find as calm and quiet a space as you can. I'm going to invite you to think of a positive memory from early life—childhood, teen years, even your 20s—so allow yourself to do whatever you need for that (e.g., close your eyes, get in a comfy spot, take a look at some old pictures of yourself). Think of a time when you felt a lot of joy—when you felt lit up inside with wonder, happiness, connection, or even simply ease and peace. If it feels okay, once you have the memory in your mind, stay with it for a couple of minutes. Notice (1) how you are in the memory, and (2) if you can notice what happens in your mind/body when you're thinking about this memory (e.g., *I'm remembering being in art class learning to make ceramics*, *I'm noticing presently my mouth forming into a smile*, *I feel a warm sensation in my chest near my heart*, and *I'm also aware that I've dropped my shoulders down into a more relaxed position*).

Please note: If you grew up in a traumatic environment or struggle to remember anything that felt positive, peaceful, or joyful, it's okay to use the first example that comes to mind even if it's more recent. If you've never really connected to joy, that's okay—the invitation is to stage some mini-experiments and notice what little things allow you to feel even 1% more at peace, lighter, or a bit of pleasure.

Next, once you've identified a positive memory, please think through the following prompts:

> In the positive memory that you identified, what did you see in your mind's eye? What were you doing? How simple or complex was the activity?

As a young person, what was a thing or things you loved to do? How did you feel when you were doing these activities? What did you think about yourself?

What is one way that you could try to incorporate something you loved as a little one into your weekly routine? It can be something very simple or seemingly small (e.g., *I loved to ride my bike so I will bike to work on Fridays*; *I got such a kick out of hula hooping so I'm going to get a couple and hula hoop with my kids*; *I'm going to set a puzzle out because I felt so happy doing puzzles with my grandmother growing up*).

EVALUATE AND PLAN TO USE THIS KEY (OR NOT!)

Below are some prompts you can use to evaluate and plan.

How was this fifth key for you? Any new knowledge or understandings? Any bits or parts you really connected with or liked? Anything you'd like to immediately return to sender?

What I took from this key and the activities was really that ___ (summarize). (For example, "I'm more likely to burn out without glimmers of joy, excitement, and pleasure in my life," or "I also can't try to force myself to be positive all the time.")

My specific plan for how I'll use this key is ___ (e.g., "I'll chat with my parent/mentor about toxic positivity," or "I'll work to intentionally add some glimmers into my daily routine more weeks than not").

Check in with yourself if it feels right to do so. Are you needing to immediately do something that counts as a glimmer for you? Clients frequently report that while at first it can feel kind of cheesy to connect with younger parts or versions of yourself, it can also be really intense and evocative. If you felt any powerful or novel feelings while thinking about childhood and early life, I'd just invite you to do whatever healthy things allow you to move through the emotions. As a therapist, it's useful when clients can identify fears, longings, and unmet needs from early life, so if you have a therapist, I'd encourage you to share with them if there's anything new on your radar you haven't processed together!

FINAL THOUGHTS

This has been the most future-oriented, forward-looking chapter in this book so far. In your current mode, what do you notice about your body, behaviors, or thoughts when asked to consider things in the future? Whatever your response—good noticing! You just had some opportunities to think pretty deeply about joy and creating a life with bits you really look forward to, savor, and celebrate.

As a species we love novelty, but change can feel hard. We're full of contradictions! Unsurprisingly, effectively managing burnout calls for some delicate needle threading and balance. You need both a felt sense of safety and predictability and some spontaneity and thrills to look forward to—you need play and pleasure, not just care and rest. Intentionally making sure that our bodies experience good things, and that we can expect more to come, is one of the surest ways to immediately address some of the most intense sensations and symptoms associated with burnout.

There's a certain element of boredom to burnout, despite fast-paced, distinctly not boring environments. It can be a side effect of sensing you don't have much to look forward to, or don't see much in the way of possibilities for growth or new experiences. As Dorothy Parker wrote in her poem, "Fair Weather" (1928): "They sicken of the calm who know the storm." In certain professions, especially those who face a lot of danger and deal with life-threatening emergencies (e.g., first responders, those deployed to war zones), a flip during burnout can happen where *everything* feels boring—even if it is objectively rather wild. It can be hard not to detach from yourself at times in roles where you're saving lives and fighting to survive. I would even argue that sometimes, it's fine and healthy for your body to click you out of having to experience certain things fully, in the present moment. In the clients I've served, I notice that one of the big reasons people end up throwing their hands up and quitting—even if they do feel aligned with their work and love so much of it—is because too much time has been spent in an agitated but bored mode. It looks like frustration and sounds like, "What's the point?"

In this chapter, you spent some time thinking about how to remind yourself—including your unconscious body—that there are good things in the world worth experiencing, worth continuing to get up and keep going for. You learned about the importance of strategizing and planning things into your routine that you look forward to, and the benefits of experiencing and cultivating glimmers. You also learned a bit more about how to appreciate the good stuff in life without toxic positivity. With the next key, you'll get to think through a number of ways to keep moving forward, if quitting isn't in the cards right now, or for a while.

KEY 6

Throw Your Hands Up Without Giving Up

> Accepting something, by the way, isn't the same as liking it. To accept a feeling that we habitually associate with discomfort doesn't mean we immediately turn around and start enjoying it. It means being okay with it as a part of the texture of human life.
>
> —PEMA CHÖDRÖN

If you know that you've got to endure a burnout-inducing role or environment, this key introduces you to some additional science and tools you can try for some relief. In my own life, I've been told either explicitly or implicitly, "Well, I can't help you if you won't help yourself," implying that I could find relief exclusively in fully uprooting or completely changing tracks: "If it's stressing you out that much—just don't do it." But I've seen some of the most stressed-out people you can imagine begin to feel a little better with a combination of some nonjudgmental connecting time with others and some therapy tools. There are some ways at least to reduce distress and reduce the risk for harm from stress, even if you have—or want—to keep on keeping on.

Key 3 gave you a chance to think through your unique situation and the options available to you right now to either slow down, step back, or walk away. Key 6 is especially for when you feel called to *stay* in an environment or stressful role that is causing you to burn out. This is also useful for creators, parents, and/or caregivers who can't—and don't want to!—remove themselves from what's causing stress. If you are a caregiver or parent, "throwing your hands up," in a health-promoting way, takes into consideration when, where, and how you're doing it, to protect the person you are caring for. Being able to manage your frustration benefits your felt sense of peace, but it also helps protect those in your care.

This chapter will help you deepen your understanding of your brain and give you some of the most effective, science-based tips proven to help reduce frustration. You will learn the main neuroscience concept and reframe that I *still* credit for helping pull me out of my worst burnout experience, and you'll get familiar with an evidence-based process called *self-compassion* that functions like a life preserver in treacherous conditions. Key 5 helped you begin to think about toxic positivity. And yet, while there are lots of unhealthy ways to try to force gratitude practices into your life, research has shown that increasing gratitude practices *can* help decrease suffering and hopelessness. Here, you'll get a chance to define for yourself and customize your own health-promoting gratitude practice(s). Stay for the whole chapter—especially if you work in health care and/or as a helper—to learn the differences between empathy and compassion, as well as some ways to reduce the risk for emotional exhaustion.

THEORY AND BACKGROUND

This chapter offers some science and practice that can help you alleviate some symptoms of burnout—especially if you're feeling impatient, frustrated, and exhausted, but you need to press on for financial and/or personal reasons. This section explores how motivation and frustration affect specific parts of the brain, as you will learn from evidence-based studies by burnout expert Emily Nagoski. Next, I'll introduce you to the science of self-compassion from Kristin Neff's research. We will finish with the *empathy dial*, an incredibly useful concept from therapist Babette Rothschild, creator of the Eight Keys series. First, let's explore some of the brain science behind motivation.

The Monitor and Motivation

There's a part of our brain that Emily Nagoski calls the "monitor" (or "discrepancy-reducing feedback loop," which can be a bit of a mouthful), which is really helpful to understand if you're experiencing intense frustration, hopelessness, and what a number of clients I've served have deemed a "f*** it!" part of themselves. Here I explain the essential bits briefly; if you want to go more in depth with the neuroscience, you can check out Nagoski's podcast (https://www.feministsurvivalproject.com/episodes/episode-08-the-monitor). This monitor in your brain is constantly tracking an equation that involves (a) what your goal is, (b) the materials or means you have at your disposal to achieve this goal, and (c) how long it reasonably should take and how long it's taking you in the present attempt. The monitor will basically get you to throw your hands up with hopelessness and frustration if it calculates that the equation is off—that you won't be able to achieve the goal, or achieve it in the amount of time reasonably expected.

Let's look at a practical example. Let's say you're going to pick someone up from a train station. It usually takes you ten minutes to drive there, and you leave so that there's just enough time to be right on time for pickup. If you depart, drive there, and it takes ten minutes like usual, the monitor is pleased. You'll likely even feel a little bit of a boost from the reward center in your brain. But now let's say, on the flipside, that you leave and halfway there you realize you forgot your phone and wallet on the counter, so you have to circle back. Suddenly, what you expected to take ten minutes is already going to be at least twenty. The monitor in your brain suddenly says, "Oh, heck no—all is lost! Goal not achieved. Screw it!" This is tricky territory. If you miss a light now, for example, you may find yourself cursing out loud instead of, say, laughing or just going on. And, I have observed that this territory has a strong chance for the snowball effect, with one frustration building after another.

So, what would reduce the frustration in this example? You'd have to intentionally, consciously shift your goal from "get to the station in 10 minutes" to "get to the station," even something like "mindfully notice a few nice or beautiful things on my route to the station." Now, of course, this is not a "just reframe things!" perspective—you and I both know this is going to be easier said than done. Learning how to *shift goals* is a huge part of walking through burnout, if you are not (yet) able to step back or stop what's burning you out.

Self-Compassion

Self-compassion scholar Kristin Neff's research caused quite a stir because she showed that, when you want to improve your performance, practicing the *self-compassion process* is more powerful than just focusing on self-confidence (Neff, 2017). I'm from Texas, where the idea that vulnerability and self-compassion can be more impactful than focusing on strength and self-confidence is certainly not the folk wisdom that gets shared. But Neff's research showed that, if you generally want to feel more capable and successful, you are not actually going to get very far standing in front of the mirror and saying a bunch of positive affirmations about yourself. Instead, Neff says, "self-compassion is a self-attitude that involves treating oneself with warmth and understanding in difficult times while recognizing that making mistakes is part of being human" (p. 141).

The three main components to self-compassion, which we will explore in the activities for this key, are these (Neff, 2017):

1. *Kindness*: "Kindness manifests as love. When our hearts are open, we can warmly embrace whatever arises in our experience with gentleness and care."

2. *Common humanity*: "Recognition of common humanity provides a sense of connection. By remembering that everyone experiences pain—that no one is perfect of leads a trouble-free life—we don't feel so alone."
3. *Mindfulness*: "Mindfulness gives us the perspective needed to present with what is, rather than contracting in fear or shame."

Practically speaking, if you're in a challenging moment when the urge might be to criticize or put yourself down, instead try an internal message like *I'm feeling sad. That's very normal and human of me. In fact, feeling this way is a reminder that I'm part of the human family. We all make mistakes—I don't have to be perfect. And I can try to be kind to myself while I'm having this feeling.*

Empathy Dial

In her book *Help for the Helper*, celebrated therapist Babette Rothschild (2022) introduced the idea of an "empathy dial." Imagine the volume knob on a record player, or something from the 1960s—it can be dialed all the way down to zero to be silent, or blasted all the way up to ten. Lower volumes are softer and gentler; louder ones can ring your ears.

Imagine blasting your empathy dial at ten constantly. Especially if you are working at something that involves caring for other humans or vulnerable creatures for a long period of time, blasting at top volume will burn you out. This doesn't mean that you never turn up your empathy, only that you have to figure out how to dial up and down with balance, so that you have something left of yourself at the end of the day for yourself and your loved ones.

DISCOVERING THE KEY

As I was completing my internship hours, excruciatingly focused on getting to that 3,000th client hour, I started coming unraveled around hour 1,200. My cynicism was through the roof—it was *dancing* on the roof. Talk therapy was helping but not really putting much of a dent in the irritating combination of apathy and frustration that was covering me all over like sap. Every morning for months I would wake up, make coffee for my partner and me, and then vent and complain to him about the exact same things in an endless loop until the coffee was gone. One thing about burnout that's rarely addressed—because typically burnout pulls our focus to ourselves—is the way it can leak onto those who love and support us—our lovers, family, children, colleagues, clients.... I was sick of feeling at my wit's end all the time and feeling guilty for basically bringing my burnout, like a third person, into my relationship. At the same time, I had to keep going if I wanted to become fully licensed and open a practice, as I had planned for so long. And the longer it took, the longer I was paying monthly dues to my supervisor. Plus, giving up would have meant going back to bartending and missing weekends with friends and feeling sleepy all the time.

That's when I first read Emily Nagoski's explanation of the brain's "monitor." Thinking back on when I finally turned that episode of burnout around, that bit of brain science was the single biggest factor in alleviating my distress. I started teaching it to clients around the same time, and I still do; you'll get to practice with your own monitor in Activity 6A.

You have read about self-compassion and the empathy dial in the theory section for this key. I'd say that, in addition to understanding the monitor, these two concepts packed the most punch with respect to decreasing cynicism and distress when my heart was hardening, and I was really starting to bottom out. Many clients also report feeling successful with self-compassion and the empathy dial, and you can explore these, too, in Activities 6B and 6D. The only other piece that stands out as especially effective is working on your relationship with gratitude, which you'll have an opportunity to think more about in Activity 6C. Research has shown that intentionally taking time to account for the good things in our lives—gratitude practices—can lead to physical and mental health benefits over time. That said, practicing gratitude without falling into traps like toxic positivity and spiritual bypassing can be tricky. Finding a balanced way through this can help with burnout distress.

What's interesting is that, when I ask people in general what they think keeps them from giving up when burnt out, the answer typically doesn't involve neuroscience but, usually, something about existential meaning and one's felt sense of purpose. I was recently chatting with my best friend, a Montessori teacher for children 18 months to 3 years old, and I asked her what she thinks keeps her from quitting when things are seriously overwhelming. Like so many of the clients I've served who work in childcare and education, she distilled it down to an inner drive that comes from feeling in alignment with her purpose—"something bigger." And she immediately joked, "But I haven't been doing this for forty years," like some of her colleagues have. If you could persist on that fuel alone—that sense of wholeness and motivation that comes from walking the path we feel is truly meant for us—you probably wouldn't be reading here now.

In Key 8 you will learn some ways to tune into and fuel up on your own "something bigger." There are times when we are burning out when apathy can overtake the usual things that energize us to keep going, so it is critical not to rely solely on meaning and purpose to keep on tract. What does help? What can help make things feel even 1% easier when you just want to give up and walk away? The following activities offer you a chance to try these four strategies on for size and see what fits for you!

ACTIVITY 6A
Work With Your Brain to Reduce Frustration

> You're burned out because this culture has messed up our priorities, not because there's something wrong with you.
>
> —JULIANA FINCH

Goal
To begin to work toward reframing your goal(s) when you are experiencing significant, disruptive distress and frustration.

Instructions
Please complete the following prompts.

> Please summarize a current main goal related to what has been really stressing you out (e.g., finish school, complete a certification, be the best parent ever, save the planet from climate crisis, finish writing my book).
>
> Thinking about your brain's monitor (your "discrepancy-reducing feedback loop"), when you feel the most frustrated and hopeless, what are you doing or thinking?
>
> How can you reframe your goal to help calm your monitor? Consider that (a) your aim is not to find a "silver lining" or force a positive perspective but to reframe your goal to be less likely to upset your brain's monitor, and that (b) this shift won't happen overnight and will take repetition and self-reminders. (For example, "Instead of counting down the hours before I'm licensed, my goal will be developing patience when there is no clear end date," or "Instead of trying to save the planet, my goal is to choose a local, grassroots effort to dedicate my time to.")

Relational Activity Add-On: Ask your partner, friend, loved one, or mentor how they would define your current, main goal. What thoughts and feelings come up when you listen to them? How do they seem to feel about your goal? What's that like for you?

ACTIVITY 6B
Self-Compassion > Self-Confidence

> At the most basic level, self-compassion simply requires being a good friend to ourselves.
>
> —KRISTIN NEFF

Goal
To explore some evidence-based ways to cultivate self-compassion and to increase focus on self-compassion practices, especially if previous focus has been on cultivating self-confidence.

Instructions
Read through the description below of six self-compassion exercises by Kristen Neff. Briefly jot down some notes about how each could look in your own life. Also note if you have already given something a serious try and it did not do enough for you.

Self-compassion has been shown by research to be enhanced through eight exercises (Neff, n.d.):

1. How would you treat a friend?
2. Take a self-compassion break.
3. Explore self-compassion through writing.
4. Supportive touch.
5. Change your critical self-talk.
6. Daily self-compassion journal.
7. Identify what you really want.
8. Taking care of the caregiver.

When is it easiest to talk to yourself with kindness, like you would a friend? When is it more difficult? Why do you suspect this is the case?

What do you think would best help you take a self-compassion break? Adding some into your schedule? Leaving a Post-it note reminder? How would this look? (For example, *for 5 minutes before our Monday meeting I'm going to set aside a few minutes to give myself a little TLC*)

Which sort(s) of writing might be a way to access self-compassion? (For example, *journaling, writing out affirmations to put on your mirror, writing letters to past versions of yourself*)

When do you feel most motivated? Least? Why do you think that makes sense, knowing you and knowing our human family?

Tip: If you're working on changing how negative and intense your inner self-critic is, it can be easier for many people to have a goal not of stopping *any* negative thought, but instead to work on adding in the self-compassion piece when you notice the harsh self-critical thought. For instance, if you think, *Ugh, I'm so lazy*, make sure to also add in something like, *Of course I'm struggling to get going—I've been overworked lately and I'm exhausted. It's really human of me to not feel intrinsically motivated by what I need to get done.*

Relational Activity Add-On: Ask your partner, friend, loved one, or mentor when they notice you being the hardest on yourself. Where do they think you could be kinder to yourself? What's a specific example? Are they invited to let you know—in a way that won't upset you—if they notice you being overly harsh with yourself?

ACTIVITY 6C
Nontoxic Gratitude

> Gratitude: the quality of being thankful; readiness to show appreciation for and to return kindness.
>
> —OXFORD ENGLISH DICTIONARY

Goal
To begin to create a sustainable practice that helps you (and your relationship or family, if you like) habitually account for what you are thankful for, without embodying toxic positivity.

Instructions
Please read through the following examples of gratitude practices, and then complete the prompts that follow.

These are examples of gratitude practices within your family or relationship. Each of these can be practiced individually as well:

- Around the table at dinnertime, or along the route home, each person shares something they are grateful for, big or small, or names one thing that was tough about the day and one thing for which they are thankful.
- When you wake up or when you go to sleep each day, list one thing you feel thankful for or appreciate.
- Make a jar for each person, or for each day, and write down at least two things you feel grateful for, related to that person or that day, and then read the notes of gratitude together at the end of the week.
- Set an alarm for yourself to remind you a few times a week to send a random text to a person you feel grateful for, to share something you're thankful for with them.
- On more days than not, create a note in your phone or in a journal listing 3–5 things you are grateful for.

- When you are saying goodnight, share one thing you are grateful for.

If you've never tried a consistent gratitude practice before, what do you think might work for you and/or your family and fit into your present circumstances? Tip: what's the simplest, fastest thing you can think of, takes minimal effort, and could be easy to add into more days/weeks?

If you have tried to establish a consistent gratitude practice before, what didn't work or help? What did you find to be more useful?

If you already have a gratitude practice that you like but you do *not* do it more days than not most months, what do you think gets in the way? What might be some work-arounds?

Have you ever tried to do a gratitude practice as a group or couple? How did that go? If you liked it but weren't keeping up with it consistently, what do you suspect gets in the way? If you have not tried it, how would that look for you?

Relational Activity Add-On: Ask your partner, friend, loved one, or mentor if they'd like to join you in experimenting with nontoxic positivity. What is a low-effort activity that you could do together?

ACTIVITY 6D
Figure Out Your Empathy Dial

Goal
To think about your relationship with empathy and compassion and to consider ways to increase balance and your felt sense of peace and spaciousness.

Instructions

Read the brief paragraph below, and then complete the prompts that follow.

In *Help for the Helper: Self-Care Strategies for Managing Burnout and Stress*, Babette Rothschild (2022) introduces the concept of an "empathy dial." Imagine a volume knob on an old-school radio or monitor that can be dialed from 0–10. As a person, if you are set to 0 on the empathy dial, you don't feel any of what someone else is feeling. If you're dialed all the way up to 10, you are empathizing with them as much as humanly possible—feeling what they are feeling right along with them. Staying dialed up to 10 all the time will burn you out. To avoid that, you have to figure out how to embody a healthy compassion and care for others that is sustainable for you and how to dip into high empathy only when needed in your role/context.

Can you tell the difference between when you are empathizing with someone—feeling a bit of what they are feeling *with* them—and when you are compassionately supporting them: feeling *for* what they're going through without experiencing through empathy the full-on emotions, sensations, and kinds of thoughts they themselves are feeling? If yes, how can you tell the difference? What do you notice about your body and mind when you're in each different mode? If no, what can you pay attention to that will help you learn the difference?

When is it easiest for you to empathize with someone? When is it hardest? When is it hardest to try to dial down how much you are empathizing with someone? (For example, "It's hardest when someone is angry and being harsh or cruel," or "It's easiest to empathize with patients going through what I've experienced myself," or "It's hardest to dial it down when it's my child, spouse, or loved one.")

Think about your role or context and the times when you are called to care for someone who is in pain and/or distress, because of work, school, or home life. Choose a recent, specific example. What would it have looked like if you had dialed empathy in to 0? All the way up to 10? (For example, "If I was at 0, I might be dissociated and numb but moving my eyebrows to look concerned—like the porch light is on but no one is home," or "I might be short and sound irritable," or "If I was all the way at 10, I might be crying along with the hurting person—they might ask me if *I'm* okay.")

If you accidentally leave your empathy dial too high for too long, what do you notice mentally? Physically? Relationally? How can you tell when it's time to think about dialing it down for more balance? (For example, "I start to dehumanize patients and see them more as bodies than people," or "I am more impatient with my kids and pets in general," or "My GI issues start acting up," or "My partner and I get into conflict more often.")

EVALUATE AND PLAN TO USE THIS KEY (OR NOT!)

Below are some prompts you can use to evaluate and plan.

How was this sixth key for you? Any new knowledge or understandings? Any bits or parts you really connected with or liked? Anything you'd like to immediately return to sender?

What I took from this key and the activities was really that ____ (summarize). (For example, "I can work with my body/brain to reduce the frustration I feel week to week, and I know that I cannot be my most empathic self 24/7 without burning out.")

My specific plan for how I'll use this key is ____ (e.g., "I won't try to stop every single negative thought I have about myself, but I will engage in self-compassion when I notice me being hard on myself").

I want to invite you to attend to your needs as you're finishing up this activities section. There are only a couple of keys left in the book! Are you needing a self-compassion break—which you now know how to do!—before continuing? If you have an intense inner perfectionist or self-critic, this chapter might have felt a bit tiresome for them. I'd invite you to give a little appreciation or gratitude to any parts of yourself that hold their nose when I talk about treating yourself like a dear friend.

FINAL THOUGHTS

A lot of this chapter is rooted in gentleness—increasing flexibility in a soft, kind way. You might have redefined some of your goals in less rigid, less perfection-focused ways. You learned the importance of increasing and cultivating self-compassion, and how you can actually be stronger and more resilient when you are less harsh in your self-criticism. You also have had space to think about gratefulness without problematic invitations to avoid or tune out difficult parts of life. And you also got to think about empathy in a less black-and-white framing that allows you to still show up compassionately, with softness when you need to, without feeling like you have to be a bleeding heart 24/7. Cultivating experiences of spaciousness and serenity is an antidote to the pressure-building qualities of burnout.

One more thought on anger and frustration: These feelings too often get talked about like they are less valid or noble in some way than more "noble" feelings like sadness. In discussing ways to reduce frustration or shift your experience, I don't want to suggest that the goal is simply not to be frustrated. Frustration, like other messengers your body uses, is there to communicate with you—to help you make sure your needs are met. There are times when anger will help you realize exactly what it is you need, or which step to take next. In this chapter I have focused more on the bang-your-head-against-the-wall flavor of frustration that carries with it fewer health-promoting possibilities. If you have worked on being aware and intentional with your empathy dial and yet you *still* notice, for instance, righteous rage shining through a lot, it's worth examining the possibility that you are in an unjust situation.

The next key goes one step farther to offer a few practical ways to cultivate (or build for the first time) some release valves to help deal with the pressure that can build up inside yourself when you are burning out. Some of you may know about putting a wooden spoon in a boiling pot to keep it from boiling over—Key 7 offers ways to "put a spoon in" your life. This will be especially helpful if you feel like you are in survival mode or on autopilot, kind of stuck or frozen, or full-on dissociating or tuning out of life whenever possible. If you have gradually become "comfortably (or *un*comfortably) numb," choosing to wake back up in the world can feel tough! The self-compassion you've practiced in this key will serve you as you move forward.

KEY 7

Cultivate Healthy Pressure-Release Valves

Choosing to laugh doesn't undermine the serious work we have to do. It enables us to do it.

—COLLEEN PATRICK-GOUDREAU

You are the sky. Everything else—it's just the weather.

—PEMA CHÖDRÖN

What happens when the pressure of stress and burnout build up inside you? One of the most common responses I hear across the board is, "I snap: I bark at my spouse when I tripped over kids' stuff. I yell at the kids over stupid things. I shout at the dog." Sometimes it's not the presence of a snap, fuss, or shout; sometimes it's the absence of our usual smile or sweetness. In relationships, acknowledgment, gratitude, and validation can stop being verbally expressed. And yet, when I make sure to intentionally release energy and pressure from my system in a consistent way, I have more flexibility: I'm able to shift gears more fluidly, laugh at myself or the situation, and think before reacting impulsively or snapping at people. There's more space within me for compassion and empathy, more bandwidth to think about the forest and not get stuck looking at the trees.

Cultivating healthy relationships and finding safe coping strategies are two of the most efficient ways to manage when you are under incredible amounts of stress and really feeling the pressure. Pressure is not an inherently bad thing, and as you've read, stress isn't, either. But it's not healthy to *stay* in a high-pressure state, without any release valves to help make sure things don't burst or explode. This key will teach you more about the science of bonding and how relationships can help protect us from the damaging effects of long-term stress. You'll learn about some of the main ways human bodies can gear up to survive when faced with a threat or the possibility of death, and you'll have a chance to think about what your own, unique nervous system requires for you to get out of that nonstop survival-mode feeling.

This chapter will also expand on the stress-response cycle from Key 4, with more focus on feelings, emotions, and your internal experiences. Research shows that it's really common for people who burn out to default to escapist coping strategies. This might look like anything from daydreaming and self-distraction to participating in events or using substances in an effort to dull, numb, avoid, or disconnect from yourself. Especially if you live in the United States, where baked into the culture are high levels of emotional and conflict avoidance—where you're told that it's bad to vulnerably feel feelings, much less share about them with others—escapism can obviously be a tempting option. Your body may even choose it for you automatically, in the form of dissociation.

To be clear, as you learned from Key 3, there are certainly times when it's healthy to *intentionally* decide to tune out and take downtime. This key can help you take an honest look at the ways you cope and provides some science-based additions and alternatives, if you feel a wish and readiness to try some changes. You'll also receive some tips proven by research to help you vent and let things out in a relationship, whether love or friendship, in ways that won't harm your bond or make one person feel overly burdened. Healthy relationships in general provide protection against burnout, so let's begin by expanding your understanding of neurobiology and bonding science. Later in this key you'll also have some opportunities to think more deeply about themes like stuckness, numbness, connection, and release.

THEORY AND BACKGROUND

Bodies in Relation

Before thinking about how your body responds when stressed and/or unsafe, let's recall what *does* make human nervous systems feel safe, secure, and capable: *relationships*. Despite the self-sufficient mythos in American culture, human beings are actually strongest when we sense that we are not alone. This does not mean that you're unhealthy if you are introverted, for example, or on the autism spectrum and have particular ways you prefer to connect. Instead, this is about knowing that, if you are ever in need, there's someone in your corner, that someone has your back. In her book *Love Sense: The Revolutionary New Science of Romantic Relationships*, therapist Sue Johnson (2013), founder of Emotionally Focused Couple Therapy (EFT, one of my preferred approaches with couples), writes: "Emotional dependency is not immature or pathological; it is our greatest strength." She used to joke that "splendid isolation is for planets—not people." Again, this is not to say that intentionally taking some space and solitude is problematic—you just need to make sure that your body also knows that you're in community, even if it's a community of two.

"I can only depend on myself" is one of the most common negative beliefs held by clients really burning out in a big way. It's a very individualistic, Western concept. Therapist Diane Poole Heller (2019), in *The Power of Attachment: How to Create Deep and Lasting Intimate Relationships*, notes:

> Couples therapist Marion Solomon writes about "positive dependency." Dependency gets a bad rap, like it's a derogatory word, but dependency can be generative, connective, and healthy. It's important that we learn to meet our own needs, of course, but we also need to receive support from others and offer to meet their needs as well. Doing so makes relationships valuable and rewarding.

Whenever I talk about the health benefits of emotional connection and relationships, I'm often met with an assumption that I'm discussing "soft science"—something kind of woo-woo or "hippie dippy." But when I'm talking about the health benefits of relational connection, of undoing aloneness, I am backed up with hard science and decades of evidence. You may recall how the Harvard Study of Adult Development showed that having a healthy bond with another person is actually associated with living longer and being less likely to experience heart attacks and stroke and to experience dementias (and get them later in life if you do). Louise Hawkley at the Center for Cognitive and Social Neuroscience at the University of Chicago even found that "loneliness raises blood pressure to the point where the risk of heart attack and stroke is doubled" (Johnson, 2008). If you think back on some of the worst-feeling times in your life so far, how much support would you say you felt during that time? If your answer sounds like, "Not much at all—I felt really alone," you're totally human.

This is not to say that you cannot feel better and begin to manage your burnout symptoms if you're in a season in life where you're more isolated. It's especially common to feel you're far away from your community when you are moving and/or changing jobs or careers, or if you are going through a training program far from home, or if you travel for long periods of time for work. Even if you're physically more isolated or alone, you can increase your felt sense of connection and community.

One caveat about this relational connection: according to the scientific evidence, if a relationship has soured (e.g., has lost trust and intimacy), this complicates things. Affective neuroscience researchers James Coan et al. (2006) wrote an article titled "Lending a Hand: Social Regulation of the Neural Response to Threat." The subjects in this study went into a stress-inducing environment—the threat of an electric shock—under three different conditions: alone, holding the hand of a stranger, or holding the hand of their spouse. Researchers measured physiological responses (e.g., heart rate, skin response) as well as subjective ratings of fear and stress. Guess who experienced the greatest amount of body activation and distress? If you guessed those who faced the threat of a shock alone, with no one to hold their hand, you are right. Participants who were holding their spouse's hand had the calmest nervous systems in the face of the threat. Even holding a stranger's hand calmed nervous systems down. However, if the quality of the marriage was low, subjects were better off holding the hand of a stranger—so it's more than *just* that there's another body there that protects us from the effects of stress!

Bodies in Danger

When do our bodies *not* feel safe? You may recall from Key 4 that your autonomic nervous system is responsible for "fight-or-flight" responses and that your body goes through the stress-response cycle by hitting the gas first and then the brakes. For the record, when there's a threat/stressor, your body can respond in more ways than just fight or flight:

- **Fight**: physically attacking the threat (e.g., punching, kicking, scratching)
- **Flight**: escaping/running away from the threat
- **Freeze**: going still and silent or completely shutting down
- **Submit**: giving in to demands of the threat without bonding or necessarily trying to please; e.g., obeying a kidnapper's orders to survive, but not becoming emotionally connected with them, or trying to make them happy

- **Attach**: bonding with the threat
- **Annihilate**: using all resources available to attempt to stand and fight and fully obliterate the threat—imagine a tiny, cornered animal viciously attacking a larger predator is has little chance of overcoming (you can read more about this response from Resmaa Menakem [2017] in his transformative book *My Grandmother's Hands*)
- **Fawn**: abandoning your own needs to keep the peace and serve/please the threat to avoid conflict (term coined originally by psychotherapist Pete Walker [2013])

Additionally, there are two kinds of freeze responses: hypofreeze and hyperfreeze. For *hypofreeze*, think of fainting goats: the dorsal part of the vagus nerve totally pulls the plug, and they fall over, with a very slow heart rate. For *hyperfreeze*, think of "playing possum": opossums stay perfectly still, but their heart rate is really high, in anticipation of any opportunity to bolt and escape.

All of these responses are normal for human bodies to experience. There's also nothing wrong with you if your body defaults to one or another. Remember that these are not necessarily conscious maneuvers—our body can go into autopilot when it perceives that it's overwhelmed, especially in isolation. This is also epically true if you survived trauma. If you're a trauma survivor, whatever you did was absolutely brilliant, because you're still here! Unfortunately, in patriarchal cultures that celebrate more masculine-coded responses like fighting, it can be all too easy to judge other responses.

Bodies in Freeze Mode

Scientists believe the freeze response is one of our ancient ancestors' first and oldest adaptations for coping with perceived threats. This is a huge broad stroke, but basically, when our ancestors were still just floating in the ocean, but other critters had evolved parts for movement—they were propelling themselves toward and eating us—we evolved an off-switch to feign death and potentially avoid being eaten.

If you are a trauma survivor, it's really normal for your body to remember sensations and thoughts from a trauma and cue a response against your will. For example, you might freeze when you smell the cologne someone was wearing when they assaulted you. When burnout fully has taken over, freezing is one of the most common experiences—often without realizing it, we come to prefer activities where we can be hanging out in the dorsal part of our vagus: shutting down, zoning out, numbing out, and even dissociating. Practically, dissociation is a mental process of disconnecting from your identity, feelings, thoughts, and memories—you "go away." In my work with couples, it's common for a partner of someone deep in burnout to say their lover feels "far away."

If dissociation is something you wish to explore more in depth, I recommend therapist Janina Fisher's resources. If you're a helping professional, her 2017 book *Healing the Fragmented Selves of Trauma Survivors: Overcoming Internal Self-Alienation* is an incredible read. Clients often come to realize through our work together that many of the activities they do outside work are just doorways into this comfortably numb place—scrolling social media, marathon TV watching, smoking a lot of weed, just generally spacing out. . . . Sometimes it's their partner or family who clues them in by complaining about feeling ignored or disconnected.

DISCOVERING THE KEY

> Emotions are tunnels. You have to go all the way
> through the darkness to get to the light at the end.
>
> —EMILY NAGOSKI

The idea of "releasing stress" has been around since before burnout was even a formal topic of study. When I noticed an uptick of clients wanting to work on burnout in counseling (especially around the first couple of years of the COVID-19 pandemic) one of the things that really caught my attention was how many skills most of these clients already had for stress reduction and management but, regardless, they *still* felt so stuck! One of the most common complaints I heard, especially from people working in helping professions with high levels of legal liability (e.g., surgeons and nurses) is that they felt they had *too much* information. They'd already attended numerous mandatory mindfulness and yoga workshops—years of trainings on burnout and self-care. But systems that benefit from your labor do not necessarily have a stake in your longevity and wellness; they benefit from getting the most out of your work during your most productive/able-bodied years. The cards are stacked against us.

I serve a lot of high-achieving perfectionists who commonly show up to therapy with anxiety and OCD. When I was first beginning to specialize in burnout, one thing that also stood out was how perplexed so many of these go-go-go types were by their new tendencies to veg out or "couch rot"—and their partners were also surprised (and often concerned) by their increased stillness. But there are different sorts of stillness. If you are being intentional and mindful, it can feel exceedingly good to be still. But if you feel unable to move out of the stillness (especially over time), it can feel more uncomfortable, like stuckness. So to be clear, there is a difference in intentionally carving out time for yourself to engage in comfy-feeling activities (e.g., "I'm going to spend the whole day watching *The Sopranos* and do nothing else!"), and it unconsciously happening *to* you, without your full awareness or consent. If you wish to work to increase your abilities to (a) recognize when you are dissociating or you've just dissociated and (b) reduce the amount of time you spend in that state, an experienced trauma therapist can help. I've also had lots of clients report that through relationship counseling with their partner(s) they were better able to practice noticing and moving through the state.

After many years serving people feeling stuck and burnt out, it's obvious to me that clients can get a sense of traction, forward motion, and release of pressure buildup even during tough times—the key really boils down to working smarter, not harder. Feeling alone or seriously lonely most of the time is like having a hand brake on in your car—you can try to go forward by hitting the gas, with yoga or mindful breathing or a $10,000 burnout retreat in Costa Rica, but if the hand brake is on, you're still not going to go very far. Building in release valves to let out built-up tension requires an awareness of our relational wiring and our need for safe connection, in addition to practical strategies to help you continue forward without just numbing out or feeling distressed and stuck.

When you're burnt out, the temptation can be to just allow the futility and hopelessness to envelope you in the darkness and to stop moving. The antidote is to "move through." As a clinician and professor, I find the phrase "get over it" useless in most cases, so I opt for *move through it* or *make room for it*. What are some practical ways to make room for an emotion, to let an emotion do its job without getting in its way or freezing up and trapping it in your body? Emotions are messages from your body like indicator lights on a car—letting you know what's needed. The following activities offer some chances to play with these concepts and think through ways in your own life to release what's weighing you down and keep connected with yourself and moving forward.

ACTIVITY 7A
Un-Becoming Comfortably Numb

> I learned how to stop crying.
> I learned how to hide inside of myself.
> I learned how to be somebody else.
> I learned how to be cold and numb.
>
> —SHERMAN ALEXIE

> Some people leave a marriage literally, by divorcing. Others do so by leading parallel lives together.
>
> —JOHN GOTTMAN

Goal

To identify if in some ways you may be (un)intentionally "numbing out" and, if you want to do some more health-promoting behaviors instead, to begin to consider some antidotes and healthy replacements and alternatives to cope that don't increase risk for harm to yourself, others, or your relationships.

Instructions

Take a look below at some common ways people shut down or tune out, zone out, or numb out, to escape being fully in the present moment in the modern world, and circle any that feel true for you sometimes or often. Then, please read the definition of *flow state* and complete the prompts that follow.

Common Ways to Disconnect, Detach, and Dissociate

- Scrolling phone or social media
- Out-of-control sexual behavior
- Marathon watching films or TV
- Sensory seeking

Consuming more porn than usual
Overuse of substances or behaviors (e.g., gaming)
Online shopping
Daydreaming or escapist fantasy

Please note: Some of these behaviors are not harmful in moderation, and in fact at times I actually invite a client to intentionally tune out the world and become absorbed in something for an hour or two. You can generally tell if something is a concern or becoming problematic if it's (a) causing significant distress, (b) being used in secret (rather simply in private), and/or (c) negatively impacting work, family, or social life.

> *Flow state*: a term coined by Mihaly Csikszentmihalyi (1990) to describe a psychological state of optimal performance, "a state in which people are so involved in an activity that nothing else seems to matter; the experience is so enjoyable that people will continue to do it even at great cost, for the sheer sake of doing it" (Beck, 1992).

As a kid or teen, what sorts of things, activities, or experiences allowed you to lose track of time because you were so purely enjoying them?

In your role or work, do you experience flow? When? How often? If not very often right now, when did you? What role were you in when you experienced it most?

If you don't experience the flow state much in your work or primary day-to-day role(s), can you think of an activity, artistic expression like writing or a craft, or game where you can sometimes lose track of time? Can you think of an easy, practical way you could add a little bit of this kind of experience to your routine, even once a week or once a month? What blocks or barriers could get in the way, and who might you need to recruit for help?

ACTIVITY 7B
Turning Into the Skid

> The body, not the thinking brain, is where we experience most of our pain, pleasure, and joy, and where we process most of what happens to us. It is also where we do most of our healing, including our emotional and psychological healing. And it is where we experience resilience and a sense of flow.
>
> —RESMAA MENAKEM

If you haven't driven in the snow, you may not know that when you start to slide you "turn into the skid"—you turn the steering wheel of your car into the direction your back wheels are sliding. If you don't, you could lose control and spin out. It might feel counterintuitive at first, but if you try to turn the other way and follow the skid, you'll end up in a spin for sure.

This is not unlike the science around emotional expression. Saying that you are sad when you are feeling sad, and letting yourself be sad for a while—that would be *turning into the skid*. Trying to force yourself to just . . . not be sad—that is actually more likely to cause a "spinout," for example, shouting at your partner or kids out of frustration, or crying in bed for your whole "day off." A spinout could also look predominantly like getting physically getting ill, such as a psoriasis flare-up or migraine.

Goal
To identify some health-promoting ways for you to experience mindfulness or to be in and aware of the present moment, and to begin to plan to consistently spend some time in the present moment week to week.

Instructions

First, please read through the following list of feelings, and think about which ones (or combinations) you have experienced in general. Then, complete the prompts that follow.

Feelings

Afraid	Embarrassed	Helpless	Out of control
Alone	Empty	Hopeful	Overwhelmed
Angry	Energized	Hopeless	Sad
Ashamed	Exhausted	Isolated	Worried
Betrayed	Happy	Joyful	

Of the above feelings, which ones are the *most uncomfortable* for you to allow to move through you, given your personality and history? It's normal if there are certain feelings and emotions you try to avoid. This may be because of accompanying physical sensations, or creepy thoughts that come with the feelings, or social stigma (e.g., contrary to your gender assigned at birth), or family or cultural messages you received about certain emotions, personal beliefs, and more.

When you look at the feelings that are hardest for you, what do you dislike about the experience of them? (For example, "I don't like to let myself feel sad because my dad told me it was weak for a man to cry," or "I don't like when my face and ears feel hot and my eyes swell when I'm crying but feeling angry," or "I don't like how people treat me like I'm fragile when I'm showing a tender emotion," or "I hate how my heart races when I'm feeling anxiety.")

When you think back on your life and growing up, was there a caregiver, sibling, or important figure who you perceived as very emotional or "big" in certain feelings (e.g., anger or sadness), who perhaps overwhelmed you at times as a kid? If yes, are there any younger parts of you who may need to hear that allowing yourself to feel those feelings won't suddenly overwhelm you? What might that part of you need from you, or need to hear from you, to feel reassured and safer?

Thinking about the most challenging feelings for you to stay in the present moment with, is there anyone or anything that helps make it easier—even 1% easier? It could be just about anything you can see, taste, smell, touch, feel, think, or believe—something as simple as a weighted blanket or glass of cold water, or a friend or partner giving you a hug or holding your hand or simply being nearby. It could even be sitting alone in your car before you go inside at the end of the day.

Are there any little gaps or small moments in your daily routine where you can just be with yourself, with no other goal except to notice what you are sensing and feeling, without judgment? If not, experimenting with even one minute a day can really be worth your effort, especially if it's something you've never tried. One recommendation I share with clients is to listen to your body and to trust yourself. If you have a goal, for instance, of sitting with yourself for 5 minutes in the morning as you drink your coffee, before you go into the kids' rooms, it can help to give yourself permission to check in before each session to see if there's any resistance. If you notice you don't want to do it, try it for 30 seconds or 1 minute. Then, decide from there if you want to do your full 5 minutes. If you start to get seriously distressed, stop and make a note. If you could do this daily, when might you try? Would it be more of a possibility weekly, or every few days?

Is there a confidant, friend, partner, supervisor, or colleague who helps you feel like it's okay to share your authentic feelings around them without stuffing or watering them down? What is it about them that makes it feel easier to fully be yourself around (e.g., personality, temperament, communication, experience, emotional expression)? *Please note:* If there isn't someone in your life right now like this, you can help meet this need by hiring a therapist—it won't be the same as a friend but a therapist can support and guide you as you build meaningful connections.

Please note: If the person who makes you feel accepted and not judged is also a solution-focused problem solver, it can be helpful to let them know that you're in a season when you just need someone to listen. You can say something like, "Before I start sharing, can I let you know if I just need you to listen and empathize, or if I want advice and help solving a problem?" When I'm working with couples, I find it broadly helpful for listeners to start listening by clarifying, "Just so I'm sure, because I want to help, do you want me to listen so you can vent, or do you want me to offer advice and help think through solutions?"

ACTIVITY 7C
The Stress-Reducing Conversation

> We can't create more time, but we can do
> less, delegate, or ask for help.
>
> —NEDRA GLOVER TAWWAB

Goal

To learn how to have a "stress-reducing conversation," an activity shown by the Gottman Institute to help partners manage stress together, and to begin to plan when you might be able to try this, or a version of this, with someone you are in relationship with.

Instructions

First, please read through the guidelines for a stress-reducing conversation, from the Gottman Institute (The Gottman Institute, 2013), and then complete the prompts that follow.

Guidelines for a Stress-Reducing Conversation

- Take turns so each person gets a chance to be the one venting.
- Avoid giving unsolicited advice or offering solutions.
- Show genuine interest in ways your partner(s) can recognize.
- Let the person sharing know that you understand by showing empathy while they share.
- Side with your partner(s), even if they don't seem perfectly reasonable (e.g., avoid or postpone saying that their boss might have a good point).
- Convey that you are a team and present a united front, that you are in it together.
- Show affection in ways your partner(s) can readily absorb.
- Validate the speaker, letting them know that they make sense to you, once they've shared.

Please note: It can help to set a timer for 5–10 minutes to ensure each person gets an equal amount of time in which to share/vent about what's stressing them out. Additionally, some people like to be empathized with as they share moment-by-moment, and others prefer for a listener to stay mostly quiet until they've shared completely, reflecting and empathizing at the end with a summary. Just make sure you know the speaker's preference when you're actively listening and working to show empathy!

Can you imagine taking turns venting like this with your partner? If it feels completely, wildly out of the question right now, think of someone who might have the capacity to share mutually about stress like this. Might a friend or colleague be willing to try with you?

What could get in the way of trying to do this together (e.g., toddlers interrupting, intense schedules)?

What might you need to plan for or do to manage or reduce these blocks and barriers? What support might you need to request (e.g., get/hire childcare for an hour so that you can be 1:1 uninterrupted or do the conversation during naptime.)?

Please note: If you try this activity with your partner(s) and things end up feeling worse, not better, or you spiral into your emotional conflict pattern, that might be an indication that individual and/or relationship counseling is needed. You might really enjoy working with a relationship counselor so that you can have help and guidance to learn how to manage together when things get tense.

ACTIVITY 7D
Cry It Out

> Anyone who says "crying doesn't solve anything" doesn't know the difference between dealing with the stress and dealing with the situation that causes the stress. Have you had the experience of just barely making it inside before you slam the door behind you and burst into tears for ten minutes? Then you wipe your nose, sigh a big sigh, and feel relieved from the weight of whatever made you cry? You may have not changed the situation that caused the stress, but you completed the cycle.
>
> —EMILY NAGOSKI

Goal

To get more comfortable with the idea that crying can be a healthy release; to begin to differentiate a big, healthy cry, like the one described above, from full-on emotional dysregulation; and to think through some ways to reduce blocks and barriers to emotional expression, especially via crying.

Instructions

Please think through and complete the following prompts.

> What did you learn from your caregiver(s) about crying as you were growing up? What messages did you receive in school? In sports or competitions? How are you feeling now remembering these words?
>
> If you grew up being told that you shouldn't cry, what did you do or try instead to move through big emotions and feelings? Are there any of these things that you *still* do sometimes, when you feel you might cry (e.g., hide in your room, run away from the house, numb yourself with substances or activities)?
>
> If, after thinking about this, you'd like to practice making more space for yourself to cry, where are places that might feel safe to do it (e.g., shower, parked car, bedroom)?
>
> Think of a time when you had a big, healthy cry that lasted around 10 minutes max. How did you feel after?
>
> If you are someone who rarely notices the urge to cry but you'd still like to explore this concept or experiment with your own nervous system a bit more, it can help to watch or experience something that historically brings tears to your eyes. Is there a song that has made you cry, or a commercial on TV? A part of a movie, or a scene from a show your kid watches? What is it about the image or sound or feel that makes you tearful? If your tears could talk, what feelings do you suspect they might describe?

CULTIVATE HEALTHY PRESSURE-RELEASE VALVES

As a follow-up to the previous prompt, if you do have a wish to explore this more, what might be a safe-feeling way to experiment with (a) allowing yourself to shed some tears, and (b) just noticing your feelings and thoughts during and after the experience? (For example, "I could watch *Inside Out 2* in private, when I know no one will be in the house for a few hours, and I can journal about the experience afterward," or "I can listen to a playlist I made during a really hard time and notice what comes up, and then share with my best friend after.")

It's important to have a backup plan as you are exploring this part of yourself. Take a minute to think about what you might try if you notice that you had been crying for longer than 10 minutes and you were beginning to feel afraid that you couldn't stop, or if you are feeling increasingly distressed or out of control. What might be a healthy distraction to get your brain focused on something else (e.g., call a friend, watch a favorite show, take a walk)? How could you change the state of your body, if this happens to you (e.g., if you're lying down, sit up, and if you're sitting, stand; take a hot bath or splash cold water on your face; step outside or into another room or seat)? Who could help you out? (For example, "I could ask my partner for a hug and some verbal reassurance," or "I could cuddle my pet," or "I can chat with my therapist.")

Please note: If you're just beginning to explore your emotional wiring for the first time and you're afraid that allowing yourself to cry might break some dam and that you could get carried away or not be able to stop, this is an incredibly normal worry. A mental health counselor can help you feel safe to experiment and practice with this—let a professional know you'd like support with *emotional regulation*.

EVALUATE AND PLAN TO USE THIS KEY (OR NOT!)

Below are some prompts you can use to evaluate and plan.

> How was this seventh key for you? Any new knowledge or understandings? Any bits or parts you really connected with or liked? Anything you'd like to immediately return to sender?
>
> What I took from this key and the activities was really that ___ (summarize). (For example, "In addition to stress-response completion, I can reduce how stuck I feel by cultivating ways to release tension and being willing to experience/move through emotions.")
>
> My specific plan for how I'll use this key is ___ (e.g., "I'll chat with my partner and see if they will do a stress-reducing conversation with me biweekly").

Since this chapter is all about built-up pressure, check in with yourself: Are you needing a little release? Knowing yourself and thinking about what you learned in this key, if you were to offer yourself a little something to help with stress before continuing on, what would it be? Please make some room to take care of what you're needing. Only one more key to go!

FINAL THOUGHTS

Choosing to be more conscious and present in the world is courageous when you're burning out. Rest assured that, even when things feel chaotic and overwhelming, or too heavy to manage, you can continue to make it easier to move forward by increasing the spaciousness you feel within yourself. When you work on your relationships with yourself and others simultaneously, you are setting yourself up for your best chance at feeling more ease and relief, as well as keeping yourself from exploding on everyone around you. This is an incredible gift to yourself, filled with individual and personal benefits as you work at remaining present, upright, and moving forward, even if you wish only to close your eyes and drift off far away into coziness of the void.

It is also an incredible gift to the world, if you're someone who wants to help create change, that can ripple out to impact our human family in profound ways. When you act to stay healthy, resourced, and thriving, not just scraping by on survival mode, you literally create new possibilities in the world. When your goal isn't to just get by but to bank a little extra for a rainy day, you can create a surplus that allows for greater flexibility in the world. When I'm feeling good—neutral, even (at least, specifically not burnt out)—it's way easier at the end of a bad day or a long week to give patience and understanding to people who may *not* be feeling so great.

What is more, when I've been consistently working at self-compassion and loving myself, it's also much easier to take in necessary critical feedback. You can grow only to the extent that you are willing to encounter and explore your shadow side, and that takes a lot of energy, curiosity, and openness.

For all these reasons, working on yourself individually for the goal of reducing burnout symptoms is actually pretty revolutionary. Successful advocates and activists can shift gears fluidly, from intentionally being still and recharging with ease to pushing forward relentlessly, dauntlessly.

The next key offers some thoughts about zooming out to consider the bigger picture, including your personal philosophy and ways of making meaning and significance, as well as society and our U.S. culture. As a white woman who works at being antiracist, it's persistently increasingly clear how the silence, inaction, apathy, and hopelessness that comes with burnout benefits those with a stake in keeping things the same, and even going back to the past when things were even less fair and just. Whatever and whoever you feel called to advocate for, you will be more effective if you know how to take care of yourself and stay open and authentic, instead of shrunken and closed down. The next and last key is all about finding ways for you to evolve, to prevent burnout in the long run, and to stand in your power.

KEY 8

Focus On Something Bigger

> A reckoning with burnout is so often the reckoning with the fact that the things you fill your day with—the things you fill your life with—feel unrecognizable from the sort of life you want to live, and the sort of meaning you want to make in it. That's why the burnout condition is more than just an addition to work. It's an alienation from the self, and from desire. If you subtract your ability to work, who are you? Is there a self left to excavate?
>
> —ANNE HELEN PETERSEN

The first key began with an invitation to zoom out and consider history, context, politics, and culture. Then, the following keys zoomed back in for you to examine your unique, personal experience of burnout and how it shows up in your body, mind, and relationships. This final key zooms back out again to help you think more deeply about such existential things as your place in the universe, your deepest values and longings, and what gives you meaning and purpose—your "something bigger." Recognizing and intentionally calling this something bigger to mind, when you're in the heaviest, most hopeless moments of burnout, can shine an almost unrivaled light for you into the darkness.

If you notice immediate frustration with any thought of an invitation to focus on something bigger, that's okay. I saved this key for last for a reason: it's the most existential, and as you've learned, you need some nervous system balance, safety, and access to the big, front part of your brain to truly be able to explore this sort of territory. I'm not saying that it's *never* useful to think about these more complex, philosophical and spiritual things during the most intense, disorienting, and distressing parts of your burnout. It's just that it would be pretty hard to do on your own while reading a book. A mentor of mine coached me to distill down things like my values, goals, and self-identified purpose—the simpler we can get it, she explained, the easier it will come to us when we're in crisis or stressed and need to make important decisions. The more our actions and behaviors in the world align with what we perceive our deepest purpose to be, the more fulfilled we'll likely be. Our *interests* don't have to wildly align with our day job to feel satisfied, but if our *values* don't, it can feel harder to prevent burnout than when someone's values align closely with their workplace.

The relationship between burnout and what generates meaning, significance, and purpose for you is an interesting one. It's often the most passionate people—the ones who feel called to what they do by whatever they see as a higher power or the universe—who actually burn out the fastest, regardless of the web of other contributing factors I've outlined. So, this key is not just about figuring out or reminding yourself of your purpose. If simply loving what we do would prevent us from burning out, I would have very few clients. It's often precisely because we love what we do so much that we get lost in the first place, or why we are willing to self-sacrifice and live a life smaller than what's possible for us: it feels simply like the price of the privilege to get to do what you feel born to do.

This chapter addresses some of these existential, more philosophical aspects of burnout. That takes a lot of energy from the front part of your brain, which you might not have if you're as stressed as can be.

It's okay if you aren't in a place right now for this kind of activity. Feel invited to take a self-compassion break if you sense any self-judgmental parts of yourself piping up. This key also gives you a chance to think more about what it means to be a part of our human family and to consider some recommendations for taking care of your whole self. Connecting all the way back to the introduction to this book, and the first key, we'll finish by considering ways you can identify and leverage your own unique combination of privilege and power, to help shift and change the exploitative, oppressive systems responsible for burnout.

THEORY AND BACKGROUND

Viktor Frankl, a Jewish therapist and researcher who was imprisoned in a Nazi concentration camp during WWII, wrote an incredible book out of this experience called *Man's Search for Meaning* (1946), which I highly recommend, regardless of your background, if you have time for a good read. Frankl offers some unique perspectives on persevering and personal power, for example,

> We who lived in concentration camps can remember the men who walked through the huts comforting others, giving away their last piece of bread. They may have been few in number but they offer sufficient proof that everything can be taken from a man but one thing: the last of the human freedoms—to choose one's attitude in any given set of circumstances, to choose one's own way.

Frankl argued that being able to physically endure suffering is not as essential as cultivating meaning and purpose. And Frankl believed meaning can come from three main sources: love, purposeful work or creativity, and finding courage in the face of adversity. During his internment, Frankl and his friends observed fellow prisoners who lost their sense of purpose for life: "The prisoner who had lost his faith in the future—his future—was doomed. With his loss of belief in the future he had also lost his spiritual hold: he let himself decline and become subject to mental and physical decay."

You've learned enough about toxic positivity to know it's unwise to read this summary of Frankl's work as something like, just accept the terrible consolation prize of a good attitude through the suffering—far from it. Having ways to stay forward-looking and in alignment with what feels like your own purpose—with what gives *you* meaning—can help keep you from bottoming out. Do not minimize your suffering but, rather, find meaning in order to transform how you're impacted by your suffering.

Is the word *sonder* familiar to you? I learned about it when I was living in Brooklyn, New York. *Sonder* is the realization that each and every random person you see is living a life as rich and complex as yours. Stepping out of ourselves in this way can be incredibly healthy and energy giving—wonderous, even.

Research also shows not only that can you look within yourself like this to experience increases in energy and zest for life, but also that experiencing awe can powerfully, positively impact us. In his book *Awe: The New Science of Everyday Wonder and How It Can Transform Your Life*, Dacher Keltner defines awe as: "the feeling of being in the presence of something vast that transcends your current understanding of the world." Keltner's research found health benefits of cultivating experiences of awe, including calming the nervous system and experiencing the release of oxytocin, a bonding and trust-promoting hormone. Other research has shown that five things can "flavor" the awe experience: beauty, threat, ability, virtue, and supernatural causality (Keltner & Haidt, 2003, p. 755). Activity 8C below will offer you the opportunity to think through ways you can personally cultivate awe experiences in your own life.

DISCOVERING THE KEY

When I ask people about the most unhelpful advice they receive about burnout, one of the top replies goes something like: "Everyone says you're going to burn out if you're not in a role/career that aligns with you personally—that is existentially meaningful to you. But I need this job to pay the bills, and I'm not qualified for anything else right now. I guess I'm just out of luck!" In life there are obviously times when you are going to be called to do things that do not 100% align with you. I honestly find that people who have a "work to live > live to work" philosophy—who work at something they aren't necessarily incredibly passionate about, and who feel they can leave work behind at day's end—struggle less with burnout. You can still have a meaningful, connected experience without feeling like you were literally put on Earth to do what you are doing.

That said, I've admittedly always identified as a live-to-work type: I derive incredible meaning from writing, teaching, and being a therapist, and I am quick to define myself first in these terms. If you are burning out and you don't really care too much about what you do, it still patently sucks, no question. But it can be especially tricky when doing what you love most, over time, depletes you. It can feel heartbreaking and confusing—especially if you dedicated time and resources to have the chance to do it, or if someone else helped make it possible for you to chase after your dream.

Part of what's tricky here is that simply figuring out what your purpose is will not keep you from burning out. You and I also live in a late stage of capitalism—we are bombarded by messages that work should wholly fulfill us. Here are some options to begin: (a) If you've *never* thought about what your purpose is—what gives meaning to your life in a real way—and you hate your role or job, a great first place to begin is to spend some time considering what your values and hopes are; (b) If you have spent a lot of time thinking about these sorts of things, finding balance is a more useful goal: your work or role doesn't have to be in perfect alignment with your values and capital-P Purpose (see Activity 8A, below), but we all need to find experiences of feeling aligned and embodying what we feel we're meant to be on a deeper, more spiritual level.

The main thing I hope you experience in this last key is a zooming back out, a considering of how tiny we are as individuals in the grand scheme of things, to appreciate the great mysteries that come along with being a human, and to feel out what *is* in alignment with our core self and what is *not*. Intentionally exploring and cultivating ways to do this big-picture kind of thinking and feeling can significantly impact your ability to effectively navigate your burnout. Activity 8D below will invite to think through some ways to leverage your individual power and privilege within society—at work, in family life, with friends, out and about in the world—to advocate for changes to the system that is burning so many of us out.

The more privileges you have, the stronger my invitation will be for you to advocate for change and justice in the world. We are collectively called to advocate and work for the changes we all need to reduce everyone's risk for burnout, and that takes time and effort. Things like advocacy and activism are gifts to the world, and those with more privilege and power tend to have more choices about how to spend that time and effort.

ACTIVITY 8A
My Capital-P Purpose

> Our jobs were never meant to become the center of us. They were never meant to be the course of our unworthiness. They were never meant to become the start and end of our identity.
>
> —ROBIN KIRBY

Goal

To begin to think beyond your current role and contemplate the extent to which you feel you are able to do things in alignment with what feels like your true, capital-P purpose.

Please note: This activity is more existential in nature, so you'll need your full attention for it. If you are feeling particularly exhausted, come back to this at another time.

Instructions

First, please tell a story about a time when you felt *most aligned* with what you feel your purpose is, or what feels *closest* to it that you've ever felt. Then, complete the following prompts.

> I felt most in alignment with my purpose—most like I was doing what I'm here on Earth for—when ____ .
>
> My main purpose in this life is to ____ (verb, e.g., *help, teach, reduce, raise, experience*) ____ (noun, e.g., *others, suffering, kind humans, awareness, beauty*).
>
> Some things that I already do or have done that allow me to actively be the person I want to be or become are ____ .
>
> How much are you *really* able to be who you feel you are meant to be in your current role or job? If the answer is not much, or not at all, where else in life are you able to embody your capital-P Purpose? Where could you possibly feel this?

Relational Activity Add-On: Ask a partner or loved one what they feel their purpose is. Would you have guessed their response? See if they can explain how they know it's what they are meant to do. What might life look like if both of you were feeling aligned and fulfilled?

ACTIVITY 8B
Core Values Exercise

Goal
To explore and identify your core values.

Instructions
This exercise, from TapRoot (https://taproot.com/live-your-core-values-exercise-to-increase-your-success/) offered by Barb Carr (April 2003), has five steps to help you identify your core values. Once you've generated your list of core values, think through the prompts at the end.

Please note: Feel invited to go with your gut on this—try not to overthink your selections.

1. Look over the list of values below, and note each one that feels really true for you.

Abundance	Calmness	Curiosity	Friendships
Acceptance	Caring	Daring	Freedom
Accountability	Challenge	Decisiveness	Fun
Achievement	Charity	Dedication	Generosity
Adventure	Cheerfulness	Dependability	Grace
Advocacy	Cleverness	Diversity	Growth
Ambition	Collaboration	Empathy	Happiness
Appreciation	Community	Encouragement	Health
Attractiveness	Commitment	Enthusiasm	Honesty
Autonomy	Compassion	Ethics	Humility
Balance	Consistency	Excellence	Humor
Being the Best	Contribution	Expressiveness	Inclusiveness
Benevolence	Cooperation	Fairness	Independence
Boldness	Creativity	Family	Individuality
Brilliance	Credibility	Flexibility	Innovation

Inspiration	Originality	Recognition	Success
Intelligence	Passion	Relationships	Teamwork
Intuition	Performance	Reliability	Thankfulness
Joy	Personal Development	Resilience	Thoughtfulness
Kindness	Peace	Resourcefulness	Traditionalism
Knowledge	Perfection	Responsibility	Trustworthiness
Leadership	Playfulness	Responsiveness	Understanding
Learning	Popularity	Risk Taking	Uniqueness
Love	Power	Safety	Usefulness
Loyalty	Preparedness	Security	Versatility
Making a Difference	Proactivity	Self-Control	Vision
Mindfulness	Proactive	Selflessness	Warmth
Motivation	Professionalism	Service	Wealth
Optimism	Punctuality	Simplicity	Well-Being
Open-Mindedness	Quality	Spirituality	Wisdom
		Stability	Zeal

2. List the values you chose above, grouping similar values together (e.g., you might group abundance with growth, or appreciation with thankfulness, or fun with humor).
3. For each group of values, select one word to represent the group (e.g., you might label fun plus humor as "happiness").
4. Next, add a verb to each label (e.g., you might choose to "promote" happiness, or "seek" mindfulness), and pick 1–3 that you feel most strongly about—these will represent your "core values."

What was is like to go through this activity? What are you feeling and thinking as you look at your final list of core values?

Think of a time when you did something that embodied two or more of these core values at once. When was it? What was the context? How did you feel?

How often does your work or role give you opportunities to feel really in alignment with your values? When might it feel like you are *not* embodying your values at work or day to day?

Relational Activity Add-On: Ask your partner what their core values are or to work through the exercise above. How similar are their values to yours? When you think about some of your bigger conflicts, did they relate in any way to a clash of values?

ACTIVITY 8C
Awe Chasing

> Time spent in nature is the most cost-effective and powerful way to counteract the burnout and sort of depression that we feel when we sit in front of the computer all day.
>
> —RICHARD LOUV

Goal
To learn and think through some ways to begin to tap into and cultivate experiences of awe and wonder.

Instructions
Read through the quotation below from wonder and awe researcher Dacher Keltner. Then, look at the list of Keltner's "eight wonders of life" that follow, and think of one or a few examples for each from your own life. If you can't think of something you've personally experienced, list something you might have an interest in trying in the future, or something you saw in a film or read in a book where someone else experienced that "wonder." Keltner says:

> Where do we find it? In response to what I will call the eight wonders of life, which include the strength, courage, and

kindness of others; collective movement in actions like dance and sports; nature; music; art and visual design; mystical encounters; encountering life and death; and big ideas or epiphanies. These wonders are all around us, if we only pause for a moment and open our minds. There are so many opportunities for everyday awe. (Kelter, 2023)

Keltner's Eight Wonders
1. Strength, courage, and kindness of others
2. Collective movement (e.g., dance and sports)
3. Nature
4. Music
5. Art and visual design
6. Mystical encounters
7. Big ideas or epiphanies
8. Encountering the beginning and end of life

Relational Activity Add-On: Ask your partner or loved one to share a memory from a time when you experienced awe together. How do you feel thinking about it?

ACTIVITY 8D
Leverage Your Power and Privilege

> You can be an introvert and have powerful conversations. You can be an introvert and use writing to disrupt white supremacy. You can be an introvert and show up to protest marches. You do not have to be the loudest voice. But you do need to use your voice.
>
> —LAYLA F. SAAD

Goal
To think through areas in life where you *do* have control/ability to impact, enact change, and give back (due to your individual privileges, your skills, your lived experiences), and begin to think through and plan some ways to build and maintain habits that drive changes to benefit our human family.

Instructions
Please read and complete the following prompts.

> What are some of the privileges you have (e.g., gender, ability status, race, socioeconomic status/class, age, sexuality, education level)? How much power do you have in your role? (E.g., "A lot—I'm the boss/supervisor," or "Not very much—I'm just an intern/temp.")

> What are some obstacles that you *don't* have to deal with that people without these privileges must face? (E.g., "I can pay out of pocket for a vaccine and don't have to go to a pharmacy my insurance contracts with," or "I don't have to wake up early to wait for the bus," or "I don't have to take on debt," or "I don't have to work while being in school.")

> What did you learn from your family/caregiver(s) about volunteering and serving others in your community? How did the people closest to you show that they cared about others? How could you tell when someone cared about you?

> How do you think your ancestors would feel about the path you are taking through life? How do you feel about that?

> What is an example of an issue related to social justice (e.g., reproductive rights, LGBTQIA+ rights, climate crisis) that is really important to you? What do you do to help in a practical way (e.g., donate monthly to grassroots organizations, raise money to host an affirming prom night for LGBTQIA+ youth, or boycott certain companies)? Especially if you have socioeconomic privilege or access to

generational wealth, how do you make sure that you put your money where your mouth is?

If money is tight right now and your way to push for change looks more like speaking out, sharing about important topics to your audience, and/or showing up to demonstrations, what feels like the most useful thing you can contribute, given what you'd like to see change?

For anyone who has never really thought much about this, what could be one thing you could try to start with that you would really like to follow through with?

If you grew up feeling burdened by the amount of service you were expected to do by your family or caregivers, what would a reasonable activity for you look like? How can you embody giving back to your community without giving more than you should to maintain a healthful balance? Which parts of you might have to work a bit harder (e.g., your self-compassion, your sense of balance) for you to avoid "lighting yourself on fire to keep others warm?"

For anyone who has worked their way to a leadership role, in your workplace, in your profession, in your community, if you were to carve out some time in your schedule, how could you support someone who is just beginning? (E.g., when I was almost done with my hours for licensure, and still volunteering at a community mental health agency, I would stay an extra hour each day to answer questions from more novice trainees.) How do you embody mentorship and advocacy in your current role?

At your workplace, do you notice any unfair practices that disadvantage certain, vulnerable people more than others? What is an example? Is there any way you can use your power to advocate for change? If it feels appropriate relationally, can you let these people know that you see what they are going through, and don't believe it's fair? How?

If you work in or from home, when you think about everything you do around the home, does it feel fair? Responsibilities and care tasks don't have to be exactly 50/50 for things to *feel* fair. Does your partner do their fair share? Do gender roles play into this? If yes, how? Does your partner know you feel this way? What's that like?

Please note: If you've read through this activity and you're thinking, *Okay, but with what time?* keep in mind that your own personal ability to give back is impacted by many things, and if you are reading this while you are burning or burnt out, this may not be the season to consider donating effort. If you are wealthy and exhausted, you can still use online donate links for organizations you love—it takes almost no time. I am a sustaining member of National Public Radio, which I love because I don't even have to think about it; it just automatically deducts each month. You can also make a budget for the year, if you wish to give financial gifts. If money is tight but you have some mental bandwidth, you can use your voice and share links and resources with your audience/community on social media. Ask a local charity or your religious institution if they can suggest some service opportunities.

EVALUATE AND PLAN TO USE THIS KEY (OR NOT!)

Below are some prompts you can use to evaluate and plan.

How was this last key for you? Any new knowledge or understandings? Any bits or parts you really connected with or liked? Anything you'd like to immediately return to sender?

What I took from this key and the activities was really that ___ (summarize). (For example, "I can intentionally connect with my big-P Purpose to energize and motivate myself when I'm burning out, but also to leverage necessary social changes.")

My specific plan for how I'll use this key is ___ (e.g., "I'll try making sure that I have at least one awe-chasing experience per month").

Last invitation to check in with yourself and just notice: how you're feeling, sensations on your radar, what you might be needing. I hope you can try to offer yourself some grace and softness if you're feeling overwhelmed! Remember that sharing with someone you trust is one of the most efficient ways to help with overwhelm. Do you have a friend or colleague who you'd like to chat about this book with? Reach out!

FINAL THOUGHTS

> Sometimes we are blessed with being able to choose the time, and the arena, and the manner of our revolution, but more usually we must do battle where we are standing.
>
> —AUDRE LORDE

As I was gathering my final thoughts here, I almost wrote: "It's never lost on me how cool it is that I get to experience awe pretty much every day as I witness people tell their stories." The thing is, when I'm burning out, that's the thing *absolutely* lost on me—it's like my awe recognizer goes offline! One of the reasons I love to teach is that graduate students have an amazing way of reconnecting me with a sense of wonder and deep appreciation—zest, even!—for the fields of psychology and psychotherapy. A "wow" from a student can often lift me up as much as at least half an hour in therapy with my favorite therapist. I feel similarly about spending time with my godchildren.

This chapter has offered you opportunities to think through some ways to enrich your life by cultivating awe and focusing on your core values and purpose in life. You also thought through some of the ways you can advocate for changes around you—in your family, your workplace, and your community and for our greater human family—by recognizing and leveraging your own personal power and privilege. Experiencing the multiple *ism*s in modern American life—racism, ableism, heterosexism, and so forth—is exhausting. Work can also be exhausting. Then on top of it all, there's caring for yourself and your family. And doing all this while navigating a changing world as climate crisis is escalating, technology is rapidly advancing, authoritarian dictators are gaining popularity, and fundamental rights and freedoms are increasingly threatened and stripped.

When I think about the students and clients I've spoken with about showing up in the world in a way that embodies justice, one of the biggest mental hurdles can be feeling like you have to suddenly "flip a switch" and become a grassroots organizer overnight, leaving everything behind to dedicate your life to advocacy—and when you are already burning out, that can feel incredibly out of reach. Instead, I recommend starting with something simple that you care about, something you can build into the fabric of your month-to-month and year-to-year rhythm. It doesn't have to be elaborate to be impactful. Doing things that allow you to feel like you're being who you are really meant to be in the world can truly help with burnout, even if you have to find these things outside and apart from work or your caring role. The same goes for doing things that allow you to remember that you're a part of something bigger than yourself, something incomprehensible or even mystical—something truly awe-inspiring.

It's also important to remember that we humans are social learners. We learn by watching others and modeling our behavior after them. If you grew up without anyone showing you that it's valuable to help vulnerable members of our human family, or how good and energizing it can feel to do so, it's okay if you need some ideas or resources. I hope that you are giving yourself lots of self-compassion as you are thinking through your ideas and feelings here. No one knows what you're going through but you, and I do not pretend to know what is right for you. I certainly don't want to add to your internal self-critical voice or to invoke any part of you that feels you *should* be doing *more*. Thinking through these pieces tends to help people move through the experience of burnout with less distress, and my hope for you, with this final key, is that you have had one or two moments of "Hm, I hadn't thought of that," or "Ooh, good question!"

Wrapping Up: Carrying on in Community

There are two types of tired: one that requires rest, and one that requires peace.

—UNKNOWN

If it feels okay, I want to invite you to just sit for a moment or so with everything you've read and all the new knowledge you're holding. If you have read all the way through the book to this point, you are now familiar with lots of cutting-edge science. You know some tips and tricks that are formally evidence based, as well as many that have been field tested in academic and therapy spaces.

There is one big piece that I want to touch on, as we wrap things up here. There are going to be chaotic events and unexpected factors in life—that *is* life. No amount of planning, foresight, or diligence can prevent heavy times and suffering.

Common things that crop up in life, and that you can be called to carry, even while trying to move through or prevent burnout:

- Births and deaths
- Divorce, breakups, and relationship changes
- Parenting and/or caregiving

- Debt, bankruptcy, and housing instability
- Disabilities and diagnoses
- Surgery, health crises, injuries, with short- or long-term ability changes
- PTSD (or childhood PTSD)
- Recovery
- Education and advanced training
- Grief and mourning
- Job transitions and losses
- Legal troubles

Moving through life's ups and downs without bottoming out into burnout calls on you to cultivate a felt sense of good-enoughness: *I am enough. I am doing enough. What I can offer is enough. My performance right now is good enough.* No one book will magically flip that switch on. For me, it took a few different therapists, some abjectly awful relationships and some beautiful ones, and honestly, more turns around the sun.

Depending on so many things, from the genes in your body to how you were raised (and how those who raised you were raised themselves), you may or may not have received some version of the message: "Just being you, as you are, is good. I love you unconditionally, even when you aren't perfect. I accept you. And I'm proud of you." If you did not get that message as a little one, you can still internalize *I am enough*. A good place to begin is to cultivate the thought, *I'm human, not broken*, when things go sideways. My greatest hope for this book is that you've read anything that helps you feel a little more normal and a little less alone. As a therapist, I bring so much neurobiology and psychoeducation into sessions because I see how much understanding and self-compassion can transform our lives and relationships. I hope you walk away from this book trusting, even 1% more, that there's nothing wrong with you if you're burnt out, that you are a really neat, perfectly unique human, responding how we in the human family respond, to a complex web of factors intersecting at a pretty wild time in history.

Let's also be real that, in our society, it can be hard to feel enoughness when, because of financial constraints, there actually is *not* enough to meet your and your family's basic needs. If you are struggling to keep the power on and put food on the table, existential questions about fulfillment, meaning, and purpose can feel ignorant, if not downright insulting. That's one of the main reasons I tried to include a variety of different approaches and tools here.

When stress and burnout are high and bodies are spending more time in those automatic survival modes, like sympathetic fight-or-flight or dorsal vagal freeze/shutdown, the more philosophical and existential tools will be least accessible and useful. The body-focused and emotionally focused activities and tools, even some of the brain and behavior tips, will be better for those actively struggling to stay above water and just make it to the end of the week. The same goes for material about boundaries and self-advocacy, and stress management in relationships—the season may not yet be ripe to fully explore the potential unlocked by these techniques. If you are currently reading this book while in the midst of a crisis, I invite you to keep it around when you've finished and, once things have settled down, return to it to see what else may be useful when you are in a different gear.

You and I most likely don't know each other personally, but if you have made it to this point, we've spent a good little chunk of time together! If you feel proud about taking this step toward feeling better, I want to say I feel proud *with* you. If you are still on the fence about seeing a helping professional like a therapist and you like my vibe, I hope you know there are lots of clinicians who think and work similarly.

If I could leave you with just one message, it would be to remind you that, in all this, *the number one enemy is aloneness*. If you are overwhelmed and feeling isolated and alone, the first place to start, as long as you are able to keep yourself and those around you safe, is to begin to undo the aloneness. Seeking out a therapist can help. Telling a trusted loved one that you are struggling can help. Reaching out to a mentor or spiritual leader can help. Get in community.

On the other hand, if you are *never* alone, and that's a big part of the problem, flex those delegating and asking-for-help muscles and get some time totally by yourself—even if it's one hour once a month. If you are mostly overwhelmed by feeling overwhelmed, begin by showing your body that you are safe, even though the stress has ancient parts of you getting ready to do battle! Doing all of this not only is a gift to yourself but will also honor those around who you love and love you, as well as your ancestors who came before you, and the community in which you live. Being kind to yourself is a gift to your neighbors and coworkers. So, my final invitation is to give yourself some serious credit: what you're doing is going to ripple out in beautiful ways.

Resources and Further Reading

Brewer-Smyth, K. (2022). *Adverse childhood experiences: The neuroscience of trauma, resilience, and healing throughout the life course.* Springer.
Butler, K. (2020). *The art of dying well: A practical guide to a good end of life.* Scribner.
Dana, D. (2025). *Glimmers Journal.* Norton.
Feiler, B. (2023). *The search: Finding meaningful work in a post-career world.* Penguin Press.
Geronimus, A. T. (2023). *Weathering: The extraordinary stress of ordinary life in an unjust society.* Little, Brown Spark, Hachette.
Gerin, C., Camahort Page, E., & Wilson, J. (2018). *Road map for revolutionaries: Resistance, activism, and advocacy for all.* Ten Speed Press.
Hersey, T. (2022). *Rest is resistance: A manifesto.* Little, Brown Spark.
Nagoski, E., & Nagoski, A. (2020). *Burnout: The secret to unlocking the stress cycle.* Ballantine Books.
Neff, K. (2021). *Fierce self-compassion: How women can harness kindness to speak up, claim their power, and thrive.*
O'Conner, K., Muller Neff, D., & Pitman, S. (2018). Burnout in mental health professionals: A systematic review and meta-analysis of prevalence and determinants. *European Psychiatry.* Cambridge University Press.
Ren, X., Cai, Y., Wang, J., et al. (2024). A systematic review of parental burnout and related factors among parents. *BMC Public Health, 24,* 367. https://doi.org/10.1186/s12889-024-17829-y
Saad, L. F. (2020). *Me and white supremacy: Combat racism, change the world, and become a good ancestor.* Sourcebooks.
Schwartz, R. (2021). *No bad parts: Healing trauma and restoring wholeness with the internal family systems model.*
Siegel, D. J. (2013). *Brainstorm: The power and purpose of the teenage brain.* Tarcher/Penguin.
Tawwab, Nedra Glover. (2021). *Set boundaries, find peace: A guide to reclaiming yourself.*
Waldinger, R. J., & Schulz, M. S. (2023). *The good life: Lessons from the world's longest study of happiness.* Simon & Schuster.

References

Abramson, A. (2022, Jan. 1). Burnout and stress are everywhere. *Monitor on Psychology, 53*(1), 72. https://www.apa.org/monitor/2022/01/special-burnout-stress

Abramson, A. (2024, Jan. 1). Hope as the antidote: Hope may be the antidote to today's chaotic world: Here's how to cultivate it. APA Monitor. https://www.apa.org/monitor/2024/01/trends-hope-greater-meaning-life.

ACE Response. (n.d.). Ace study. Ace Response. http://www.aceresponse.org/who_we_are/ACE-Study_43_pg.html

Adriaenssens, J., De Gucht, V., & Maes, S. (2015). Determinants and prevalence of burnout in emergency nurses: A systematic review of 25 years of research. *International Journal of Nursing Studies, 52*(2), 649–661.

Bährer-Kohler, S. (Ed.). (2013). *Burnout for experts: Prevention in the context of living and working.* Springer. https://doi.org/10.1007/978-1-4614-4391-9

Calhoun, A. (2017, Oct. 17). The new midlife crisis: Why (and how) it's hitting Gen X women. *Oprah.com.* https://www.oprah.com/sp/new-midlife-crisis.html.

Calhoun, A. (2020). *Why we can't sleep: women's new midlife crisis.* Grove Press.

Carr, B. (2003, April). *Live your core values: Exercise to increase your success.* Taproot. http://www.taproot.com/live-your-core-values-exercise-to-increase-your-success.

Centers for Disease Control and Prevention. (2021, August 23). Adverse childhood experiences (ACES). U.S. Centers for Disease Control and Prevention. https://www.cdc.gov/vitalsigns/aces/index.html

Centers for Disease Control and Prevention. (2024, April 8). *Women's health: Working together to reduce black maternal mortality.* U.S. Centers for Disease Control and Prevention. https://www.cdc.gov/womens-health/features/maternal-mortality.html#:~:text=Black%20women%20are%20three%20times,structural%20racism%2C%20and%20implicit%20bias.

Ciciolla, L., & Luthar, S. S. (2019). Invisible household labor and ramifications for adjustment: Mothers as captains of households. *Sex Roles, 81*, 467–486.

Coan, J. A., Schaefer, H. S., & Davidson, R. J. (2006). Lending a hand: Social regulation of the neural response to threat. *Psychological Science, 17*(12), 1032–1039. https://doi.org/10.1111/j.1467-9280.2006.01832.x

Crenshaw, K. (1989). *Demarginalizing the intersection of race and sex: A Black feminist critique of antidiscrimination doctrine, feminist theory and antiracist politics*. University of Chicago Legal Forum, *1989*(1), 139–167.

Cronholm, P. F., Forke, C. M., Wade, R., Bair-Merritt, M. H., Davis, M., Harkins-Schwarz, M., Pachter, L. M., & Fein, J. A. (2015). Adverse Childhood Experiences: Expanding the Concept of Adversity. American journal of preventive medicine, *49*(3), 354–361. https://doi.org/10.1016/j.amepre.2015.02.001

Csikszentmihalyi, M. (1990). Flow: The psychology of optimal experience. *Journal of Leisure Research, 24*(1), 93–94. https://doi.org/10.1080/00222216.1992.11969876

Dana, D. (2018). *Polyvagal theory in therapy*. Norton.

Dana, D. (2020). *Polyvagal flip chart: Understanding the science of safety*. Norton.

Dana, D. (2021). *Anchored: How to befriend your nervous system using polyvagal theory*. Sounds True Adult.

Felitti, V. J., Anda, R. F., Nordenberg, D., Williamson, D. F., Spitz, A. M., Edwards, V., Koss, M. P., & Marks, J. S. (1998). Relationship of childhood abuse and household dysfunction to many of the leading causes of death in adults: The Adverse Childhood Experiences (ACE) Study. American Journal of Preventive Medicine, *14*(4), 245–258. https://doi.org/10.1016/S0749-3797(98)00017-8

Figley, C. R., & Roop, R. G. (2006). *Compassion fatigue in the animal-care community*. Humane Society Press.

Fisher, J. (2017). *Healing the fragmented selves of trauma survivors: Overcoming internal self-alienation*. Routledge.

Frankl, V. (1946). *Man's search for meaning*. Beacon Press.

Freudenberger, H. J. (1974). Staff burn out. *Journal of Social Issues, 30*(1), 159–165. https://doi.org/10.1111/j.1540-4560.1974.tb00706.x

Freudenberger, H., & Richelson, G. (1980). *Burn out: The high cost of high achievement: What it is and how to survive it*. Bantam Books.

Ginoux, C., Isoard-Gautheur, S., & Sarrazin, P. (2021). "What did you do this weekend?" Relationships between weekend activities, recovery experiences, and changes in work-related well-being. *Applied Psychology: Health and Well-Being, 13*(4), 798–816. https://doi.org/10.1111/aphw.12272

Goodman, W. (2022). *Toxic positivity: Keeping it real in a world obsessed with being happy*. TarcherPerigee.

The Gottman Institute. (2013, June 21). How to have a stress-reducing conversation: Easy straight-forward instructions for having a stress-reducing conversation. *The Gottman Relationship Blog*. https://www.gottman.com/blog/how-to-stress-reducing-conversation/

Gottman, J. M., & Silver, N. (2015) *The seven principles for making marriage work: A practical guide from the country's foremost relationship expert*. Harmony.

Groenewal, P. H., Putrino, D., & Norman, M. R. (2021). Burnout and Motivation in Sport. Psychiatr *Clin North Am. 44*(3), 359–372. https://doi.org/10.1016/j.psc.2021.04.008. Epub 2021 Jul 6. PMID: 34372993.

Gungor, M. (2012). *The crowd, the critic, and the muse: A book for creators*. Woodsley.

REFERENCES

Harvard Study of Adult Development. (n.d.). Online document. https://www.adultdevelopmentstudy.org.

Hauri, P. (1996). *No more sleepless nights: A proven program to conquer insomnia.* Wiley.

Hedrick, A., Lynch, A., & Russ, A. C. (2023). Adverse childhood experiences and burnout in athletic trainers: An exploratory study. *J Athl Train. 58*(10), 876–881. https://doi.org/10.4085/1062-6050-0545.22. PMID: 37115011; PMCID: PMC11215707.

Heller, D. P. (2019). *The power of attachment: How to create deep and lasting intimate relationships.* Sounds True.

Hersey, T. (2022). *Rest is resistance: A manifesto.* Little, Brown Spark.

Hold-Lunsta, J., Smith, T. B., & Layton, J. B. (2010). Social relationships and mortality risk: A meta-analytic review. *PLOS Medicine, 7*, e1000316. https://doi.org/10.1371/journal.pmed.1000316

hooks, b. (2004). *The will to change: Men, masculinity, and love.* Washington Square Press.

Hou, T., Zhang, T., Cai, W., et al. (2020). Social support and mental health among health care workers during coronavirus disease 2019 outbreak: A moderated mediation model. *PLOS One, 15*, e0233831. https://doi.org/10.1371/journal.pone.0233831

Johns Hopkins Bayview. (n.d.) Causes and symptoms of caregiver burnout. Johns Hopkins Medicine. https://www.hopkinsmedicine.org/about/community-health/johns-hopkins-bayview/services/called-to-care/causes-symptoms-caregiver-burnout

Johnson, S. (2008). *Hold me tight: Seven conversations for a lifetime of love.* Little, Brown.

Johnson, S. (2013). *Love sense: The revolutionary new science of romantic relationships.* Little, Brown.

Joinson, C. (1992). Coping with compassion fatigue. *Nursing, 22*, 116, 118–120.

Jovanović, N., Podlesek, A., Volpe, U., et al. (2016). Burnout syndrome among psychiatric trainees in 22 countries: Risk increased by long work hours, lack of supervision, and psychiatry not being first career choice. *European Psychiatry, 32*, 34–41.

Kahneman, D., & Deaton, A. (2010). High income improves evaluation of life but not emotional well-being. *Proceedings of the National Academy of Sciences of the United States of America, 107*(38), 16489–16493. https://doi.org/10.1073/pnas.1011492107

Kancherla, B. S., Upender, R., Collen, J. F., et al. (2020). What is the role of sleep in physician burnout? *Journal of Clinical Sleep Medicine, 16*(5), 807–810.

Keltner, D., & Haidt, J. (2003). Approaching awe, a moral, spiritual, and aesthetic emotion. *Cognition and Emotion, 17*(2), 297–314. https://doi.org/10.1080/02699930302297

Keltner, D. (2023). *Awe: The new science of everyday wonder and how it can transform your life.* Penguin Press.

Kendi, I. X. (2019). *How to be an antiracist.* One World.

Leone, S., Wessely, S., Huibers, M. J. H., et al. (2011). The sides of the same coin? On the history and phenomenology of chronic fatigue and burnout. *Psychology and Health, 26*, 449–464.

Maslach, C., & Jackson, S. E. (1981). *Maslach Burnout Inventory—ES Form (MBI)* [Database record]. APA PsycTests. https://doi.org/10.1037/t05190-000

Mayo Clinic Staff. (2023, August 9). *Caregiver stress: Tips for taking care of yourself.* Mayo Clinic. https://www.mayoclinic.org/healthy-lifestyle/stress-management/in-depth/caregiver-stress/art-20044784

Mayo Clinic Staff. (2023, Nov. 30). *Job burnout: How to spot it in action.* Mayo Clinic. https://www.mayoclinic.org/healthy-lifestyle/adult-health/in-depth/burnout/art-20046642

Menakem, R. (2017). *My grandmother's hands: Racialized trauma and the pathway to mending our hearts and bodies.* Central Recovery Press.

McKee-Lopez, G., Robbins, L., Provencio-Vasquez, E., & Olvera, H. (2019). The relationship of childhood adversity on burnout and depression among BSN Students, *Journal of Professional Nursing*, *35*(2), 112–119. https://doi.org/10.1016/j.profnurs.2018.09.008

Mikkola, L., Suutala, E., & Parviainen, H. (2018). Social support in the workplace for physicians in specialization training. *Medical Education*, *23*, 1–10. https://doi.org/10.1080/10872981.2018.1435114

Nagoski, E., & Nagoski, A. (2020). *Burnout: The secret to unlocking the stress cycle*. Ballantine Books.

Neff, K. (2015). *Self-compassion: The proven power of being kind to yourself*. William Morrow.

Neff, K. (2017, Dec. 28). Why self-compassion beats self-confidence. *The New York Times*. https://www.nytimes.com/2017/12/28/smarter-living/why-self-compassion-beats-self-confidence.html.

Neff, K. (n.d.). *Self-compassion practices*. Self-Compassion, Dr. Kristin Neff. https://self-compassion.org/self-compassion-practices/

Okun, T., & Jones, K. (2001). *Dismantling racism workbook*. Dismantlingracism.org.

Pagnin, D., de Queiroz, V., Carvalho, Y. T. M. S., et al. (2014). The relation between burnout and sleep disorders in medical students. *Academic Psychiatry*, *38*, 438–444. https://doi.org/10.1007/s40596-014-0093-z

Parker, D. (1928). Fair weather. In *Sunset gun: Poems by Dorothy Parker* (p. 50). Boni & Liveright.

Porges, S. W. (2011). *The polyvagal theory: Neurophysiological foundations of emotions, attachment, communication, and self-regulation*. Norton.

Prinz, P., Hertrich, K., Hirschfelder, U., et al. (2012). Burnout, depression and depersonalisation—psychological factors and coping strategies in dental and medical students. *GMS Zeitschrift für Medizinische Ausbildung*, *29*(1), Doc10. https://doi.org/10.3205/zma000780

Raymaker, D. M., Teo, A. R., Steckler, N. A., et al. (2020). Having all of your internal resources exhausted beyond measure and being left with no clean-up crew: Defining autistic burnout. *Autism Adulthood*, *2*(2), 132–143. https://doi.org/10.1089/aut.2019.0079

Resch, E., & Tylka, T. L. (2019). Intuitive eating. In T. L. Tylka & N. Piran (Eds.), *Handbook of positive body image and embodiment: Constructs, protective factors, and interventions*, 68–79. Oxford University Press. https://doi.org/10.1093/med-psych/9780190841874.003.0008

Rosen, D., & Suni, E. (2024, March 4). Mastering sleep hygiene: Your path to quality sleep. *The Sleep Foundation*. http://www.sleepfoundation.org/sleep-hygiene.

Rosenbloom, S. (2010, Aug. 7). But will it make you happy? *The New York Times*. https://www.nytimes.com/2010/08/08/business/08consume.html.

Roskam, I., Brianda, M. E., & Mikolajczak, M. (2018). A step forward in the conceptualization and measurement of parental burnout: The Parental Burnout Assessment (PBA). *Frontiers in Psychology*, *9*, 758.

Rothschild, B. (2022). *Help for the helper: Preventing compassion fatigue and vicarious trauma in an ever-changing world*. Norton.

Ruisoto, P., Ramírez, M. R., García, P. A., et al. (2021). Social support mediates the effect of burnout on health in health care professionals. *Frontiers in Psychol*, *11*, 623587. https://doi.org/10.3389/fpsyg.2020.623587

Sandberg, S., and Grant, A. (2017). *Option b: Facing adversity, building resilience, and finding joy*. Knopf.

REFERENCES

Sawhney, V. (2020, Nov. 10). It's okay to not be okay. *Harvard Business Review*. https://hbr.org/2020/11/its-okay-to-not-be-okay.

Schabram, K., Bloom, M., & DiDonna, D. J. (2023). Recover, explore, practice: The transformative potential of sabbaticals. *Academy of Management Discoveries, 9*(4). https://doi.org/10.5465/amd.2021.0100

Schwartz, R. (1997). *Internal family systems therapy*. Guilford Press.

Schwartz, R. (2017). *Internal family systems skills training manual: Trauma-informed treatment for anxiety, depression, PTSD, and substance abuse*. PESI Publishing & Media.

Schwartz, R. (2019). *Internal family systems therapy*. The Guilford Press.

Schweitzer, G. (2016). *Rewiring tinnitus: How I finally found relief from the ringing in my ears*. CreateSpace Independent Publishing Platform.

Siegel, D. (2013). *Brainstorm: The power and purpose of the teenage brain*. TarcherPerigee.

Siegel, D. J. (n.d.).The healthy mind platter. Online document. https://drdansiegel.com/healthy-mind-platter/

Söderström, M., Ekstedt, M., Jeding, K., et al. (2012). Insufficient sleep predicts clinical burnout. *Journal of Occupational Health Psychology, 17*(2), 175–183. https://citeseerx.ist.psu.edu/document?repid=rep1&type=pdf&doi=ffb7eadfc27740b203e26d80af1cdb9ea9469cbc

Stoewen, D. L. (2019). Moving from compassion fatigue to compassion resilience, part 2: Understanding compassion fatigue. *Canadian Veterinary Journal, 60*(9), 1004–1006.

Talavera-Velasco, B., Luceño-Moreno, L., Martín-García, J., et al. (2018). Psychosocial risk factors, burnout and hardy personality as variables associated with mental health in police officers. *Frontiers in Psychology, 9*. https://doi.org/10.3389/fpsyg.2018.01478

Toker, S., & Melamed, S. (2017). Stress, recovery, sleep, and burnout. In C. L. Cooper & J. C. Quick (Eds.), *The handbook of stress and health: A guide to research and practice* (ch. 10). Wiley.

Tribole, E., & Resch. E. (2020). *Intuitive eating: A revolutionary anti-diet approach*. 4th ed. St. Martin's.

Trockel, M. T., West, C. P., Dyrbye, L. N., et al. (2023). Assessment of adverse childhood experiences, adverse professional experiences, depression, and burnout in US physicians. *Mayo Clinic Proceedings, 98*(12), 1785–1796. https://doi.org/10.1016/j.mayocp.2023.03.021

Welwood, J. (2024, Feb. 10). On spiritual bypassing and relationship. https://scienceandnonduality.com/article/on-spiritual-bypassing-and-relationship/

World Health Organization (WHO). (1993). *The ICD-11 classification of mental and behavioral disorders*. World Health Organization.

World Health Organization (WHO). (2019). Burn-out an "occupational phenomenon": International Classification of Diseases. https://www.who.int/news/item/28-05-2019-burn-out-an-occupational-phenomenon-international-classification-of-diseases

Yellowlees, P., Coate, L., Misquitta, R., Wetzel, A. E., & Parish, M. B. (2021). The association between adverse childhood experiences and burnout in a regional sample of physicians. [Abstract.] *Academic Psychiatry: the Journal of the American Association of Directors of Psychiatric Residency Training and the Association for Academic Psychiatry, 45*(2), 159–163. https://doi.org/10.1007/s40596-020-01381-z

Index

A Burnt-Out Case, 36
abuse
   childhood. *see* childhood abuse
accomplishments
   decreased sense of, 36
Accountability Partners activity, 53–55
   goal, 53
   instructions, 54–55
ACEs. *see* adverse childhood experiences (ACEs)
activity(s)
   burnout-related. *see specific types and* burnout activities
adult health risk behaviors
   ACEs and, 11–14
   childhood abuse/household dysfunction and, 11–14
adult life
   Harvard Adult Development Study on, 10–11
Adverse Childhood Experience Questionnaire for Adults, 23–27
   Expanded ACE Checklist, 25
   goal, 24
   instructions, 24–27
   Original ACE Checklist, 24–25
adverse childhood experiences (ACEs)
   adult health risk behaviors related to, 11–14
   burnout related to, 12–14
   CDC on, 12–13
   questionnaire for adults, 23–27. *see also* Adverse Childhood Experience Questionnaire for Adults
   types of, 12
Adverse Childhood Experiences (ACE)
   study, 12
Alexie, S., 144
aloneness
   burnout related to, 14–16
   as enemy, 177–78
American Journal of Preventative Medicine, 12
annihilate
   described, 140
attach
   described, 140
autistic burnout
   described, 41
autonomic ladder, 102, 103*f*
autonomic nervous system, 100
awareness
   self-. *see* self-awareness
Awe: The New Science of Everyday Wonder and How It Can Transform Your Life, 160
Awe Chasing activity, 166–67
   goal, 166
   instructions, 166–67

balance
  described, 79–80
behavior(s)
  adult health risk. *see* adult health risk behaviors
  burnout-related, 50
Big Breaks and Little Rests activity, 68–70
  goal, 68
  instructions, 68–70
birth(s)
  CDC on deaths related to giving, 5–6
Bloom, M., 61–62
body(ies)
  in danger, 139–40
  in freeze mode, 140–41
  in relation, 137–39
brain
  monitor in, 121–22, 124
  in motivation, 121–22
brain integration
  defined, 68
break-taking
  burnout-related, 61–66
burnout
  ACEs and, 12–14
  activities in managing. *see* burnout management; *specific types and* burnout activities
  aloneness and, 14–16
  aspects of, 36
  assessment of, 3–4, 36–37
  autistic, 41
  avoiding, 59–77. *see also* learning when/how to slow down, step back, and walk away
  behaviors/symptoms, 50
  break-taking related to, 61–66
  as buzzword, xxvii
  candidates for, xiv, xxii–xxiii, 6–7
  characteristics of activities that most impact renewal/recovery from, 93–95
  cultivating healthy pressure-release valves for, 135–56. *see also* cultivating healthy pressure-release valves
  danger rating related to, 47–53, 48*f. see also* My Burnout Danger Rating activity
  defined, 37, 38*f*
  described, xiv, xix, 36–37
  emergency resources, xxxii–xxxiii
  emotions/feelings, 51
  factors influencing, 14–16
  flourishing vs., xix
  focusing on something bigger, 157–73
  healing from, 34, 59–77
  historical timeline related to, 38
  how to work smarter, not harder in preventing, xxi
  human needs and, 8–11
  ICD-11 on, 37, 38*f*
  identifying/appreciating your own social, cultural, and psychological risks related to, 3–31. *see also* identifying/appreciating your own social, cultural, and psychological risks
  intersectionality in examination of, xxviii–xxix
  isolation and, 11
  learning when/how to slow down, step back, and walk away in, 59–77
  loneliness and, 14–16
  management of, 14–16. *see* burnout management
  Mayo Clinic on, 38*f*
  MBI in assessment of, 36–37
  medical diagnoses related to, 6
  perfectionism and, 9
  power impact on, 5, 8
  prevalence of, xiv
  prevention of, 99–117. *see also* figuring out what keeps your fire going
  privilege impact on, 5, 8
  recognizing when you are careening toward, 33–57. *see also under* recognizing when you are careening toward burnout
  recovery from, 64–66, 93–95. *see also* burnout recovery
  relationship between what generates meaning, significance, and purpose for you and, 158
  risk-level warning sign for, 47–49, 48*f*
  self-awareness impact of, 33
  self-care related to, xix–xx
  "simple" things become big things in, 5–6
  sleep deficit impact on, 62–63
  social support in preventing, 10–11
  sources of, xxiii
  stress related to, 79–97. *see also* doing something with the stress
  thriving vs., xix
  throwing your hands up without giving up vs., 119–34. *see also* throwing your hands up without giving up
  types of, 36–37

INDEX

unexpected factors in life impacting, 175–76
what it feels like, 39–40
in working parent/caregiver, 6–7
burnout activities. *see also specific types*
  cultivating healthy pressure-release valves activities, 144–53
  described, 16
  doing something with the stress activities, 85–87
  figuring out what keeps your fire going activities, 108–15
  focusing on something bigger activities, 162–70
  identifying/appreciating your own social, cultural, and psychological risks activities, 16–29
  learning when/how to slow down, step back, and walk away, 66–75
  recognizing when you are careening toward burnout–related, 42–55
  throwing your hands up without giving up activities, 126–32
burnout management
  practicing saying "no" in, 63
burnout recovery
  components of, xxv–xxvii
  goals in, xxv–xxvi
  markers in gauging success in, xxv–xxvi
  modifications to work environment in, xxvi
Burnout Risk-Factor Checklist, 17–21
  caregiving-related, 19
  employment-related, 17–18
  goal, 17
  instructions, 17–21
  journaling prompts, 20–21
burnt out
  as exploited, 8
bypassing
  spiritual, 105

Calhoun, A., 70
capitalism
  impact on citizens' lives, 7–8
care
  self-. *see* self-care
caregiver(s)
  burnout among, 6–7
  stress of. *see* caregiver stress
  types of, 6
caregiver stress
  signs of, 35

caregiving
  Burnout Risk-Factor Checklist related to, 19
Carr, B., 164
CDC. *see* Centers for Disease Control and Prevention (CDC)
Center for Cognitive and Social Neuroscience
  at University of Chicago, 138
Centers for Disease Control and Prevention (CDC)
  on ACEs, 12–13
  on birth-related deaths, 5–6
  on links between adult health risk behaviors and childhood abuse/household dysfunction, 11–14
certainty
  as human need, 9–10
Chemaly, S., 70
childhood abuse
  adult health risk behaviors related to, 11–14
Chödrön, P., 119, 135
Clarke, S., 66
Coan, J. A., 139
Coming Up for Air activity, 93–95
  goal, 93
  instructions, 93–95
common humanity
  in self-compassion, 123
community(ies)
  carrying on in, 175–77
compassion
  self-. *see* self-compassion
connection
  forms of, 11
  as human need, 9–11
Cons and Cons list, 72–75
contribution
  as human need, 9–11
control
  in renewal/recovery from burnout, 94
conversation
  stress-reducing, 149–51. *see also* stress-reducing conversation; The Stress-Reducing Conversation activity
Copeland, K., 72
Copenhagen Nature and Medical Library, xiv
coping strategies
  safe, 136
core-self energy
  recognizing one's, 44–46

core values
  exploring/identifying, 164–66
Core Values Exercise, 164–66
  goal, 164
  instructions, 164–66
Crenshaw, K., xxviii
Cry It Out activity, 151–53
  goal, 152
  instructions, 152–53
Csikszentmihalyi, M., 145
cultivating healthy pressure-release valves, 135–56
  activities for, 144–53. *see also specific types and* cultivating healthy pressure-release valves activities
  bodies in danger, 139–40
  bodies in freeze mode, 140–41
  bodies in relation, 137–39
  discovering, 141–43
  evaluate/plan for use, 154
  final thoughts, 154–56
  introduction, 135–37
  theory/background, 137–41
cultivating healthy pressure-release valves activities, 144–53
  Cry It Out activity, 151–53
  The Stress-Reducing Conversation activity, 149–51
  Turning Into the Skid activity, 146–49
  Un-Becoming Comfortably Numb activity, 144–45
cultural risks
  identifying/appreciating one's own, 3–31. *see also* identifying/appreciating your own social, cultural, and psychological risks
cultural values
  toxic, 27–28. *see also* Inventory of Toxic Cultural Values activity
culture
  grind. *see* grind culture

Dana, D., 100, 102, 103*f,* 112–13
  Polyvagal Ladder of, 102, 103*f*
danger
  bodies in, 139–40
  burnout-related, 47–53, 48*f. see also* My Burnout Danger Rating activity
"Dan Siegel hand-brain model video," 88
DeBotton, A., 99
decreased sense of accomplishment
  burnout-related, 36

"Demarginalizing the Intersection of Race and Sex," xxviii
dependency
  "positive," 138
depersonalization
  burnout-related, 36
detaching
  common methods of, 144–45
detachment
  in renewal/recovery from burnout, 93
DiDonna, D. J., 61–62
Discernment–When to Walk Away activity, 72–75
  goal, 72
  instructions, 72–75
disconnecting
  common methods of, 144–45
Dismantling Racism Workbook, 27–28
dissociating
  common methods of, 144–45
Dodge Toxic Positivity activity, 109–12
  goal, 109
  instructions, 109–12
doing something with the stress, 79–97
  activities for, 85–95. *see also specific types and* doing something with the stress activities
  discovering, 84–85
  evaluate/plan for use, 95
  final thoughts, 96–97
  introduction, 79–81
  theory/background, 81–84
doing something with the stress activities, 85–95
  Coming Up for Air activity, 93–95
  Joyful Movement and Exercise activity, 90–93
  Name It to Tame It activity, 88–90
  Seven Ways to Complete the Stress-Response Cycle activity, 85–87

EFT. *see* Emotionally Focused Couple Therapy (EFT)
"Eight Cs of Self," 44–46
"eight wonders of life"
  Keltner's, 166–67
emergency resources
  burnout-related, xxxii–xxxiii
emotion(s)
  burnout-related, 51
emotional attunement
  burnout related to, 14–16

INDEX

emotional exhaustion
  burnout-related, 36
emotional expression
  described, 16
Emotionally Focused Couple Therapy (EFT), 137
empathy dial
  in throwing your hands up without giving up, 123
employment
  Burnout Risk-Factor Checklist related to, 17–18
energy
  core-self, 44–46
environment
  work-related, xxvi
exhaustion
  emotional. *see* emotional exhaustion
Expanded ACE Checklist, 25
experience(s)
  internal. *see* internal experiences
exploited
  burnt out as, 8
expression
  emotional. *see* emotional expression

"Fair Weather," 116
family(ies)
  grind culture in, 21–23. *see also* The Story of Grind Culture in My Family activity
fawn
  described, 140
feeling(s)
  burnout-related, 51
  types of, 147
fight
  described, 139
Figley, C. R., 38*f*
Figure Out Your Empathy Dial activity, 130–32
  goal, 130
  instructions, 131–32
figuring out what keeps your fire going, 99–117
  activities for, 108–15. *see also specific types and* figuring out what keeps your fire going activities
  discovering, 106–7
  evaluate/plan for use, 115–16
  final thoughts, 116–17
  introduction, 99–101

  theory/background, 101–6, 103*f*
  figuring out what keeps your fire going activities, 108–15
    Dodge Toxic Positivity activity, 109–12
    Glimmers and Triggers activity, 112–13
    Reconnect With What Lights You Up activity, 113–15
    Something to Look Forward to activity, 108–9
Finch, J., 3, 126
fire
  figuring out what keeps yours' going, 99–119. *see also* figuring out what keeps your fire going
Fisher, J., 141
flexibility
  building of, 100
flight
  described, 139
flourishing
  burnout vs., xix
  described, xix
flow state
  described, 145
focusing on something bigger, 157–73
  activities for, 162–70. *see also specific types and* focusing on something bigger activities
  discovering, 161–62
  evaluate/plan for use, 170–71
  final thoughts, 171–73
  introduction, 157–59
  theory/background, 159–60
focusing on something bigger activities, 162–70
  Awe Chasing activity, 166–67
  Core Values Exercise, 164–66
  Leverage Your Power and Privilege activity, 167–70
  My Capital-P Purpose activity, 162–63
Frankl, V., 159–60
free dives
  defined, 69
freeze
  described, 139
freeze mode
  bodies in, 140–41
Freudenberger, H., xxii, 36, 38*f*

Ginoux, C., 93–94
giving birth
  CDC on deaths related to, 5–6

glimmer(s)
  defined, 113
  examples of, 113
  triggers vs., 100–1
Glimmers and Triggers activity, 112–13
  goal, 112
  instructions, 112–13
Goines, V., Rev., 90
Goodman, W., 105–6
Gottman Institute, 149–50
Gottman, J. M., 144
gratitude
  defined, 129
  Oxford English Dictionary on, 129
gratitude practices
  types of, 129–30
Greene, G., 35–36
grind culture
  described, 21
growth
  as human need, 9–11
Gungor, M., xxi

Harvard Study of Adult Development, xxxi, 10–11, 138
Hauri, P., 62
Hawkley, L., 138
healing
  from burnout, 34, 59–77
Healing the Fragmented Selves of Trauma Survivors: Overcoming Internal Self-Alienation, 141
Healthy Mind Platter activity, 66–68
  goal, 67
  instructions, 67–68
healthy relationships
  cultivating, 136
Heaney, S., 99
Heller, D. P., 137–38
Hellman, C., 101
Help for the Helper: Self-Care Strategies for Managing Burnout and Stress, xv, 123, 131
helpful positivity
  qualities of, 105–6
  toxic positivity vs., 105–6
Henson, J., 113
Hersey, T., xxvii, 21, 53, 59, 63–64
holidays
  working, 69
homeostasis
  defined, 79–80

hooks, b., 13
hope
  described, 101
  wishing vs., 101
Hope Research Center
  at University of Oklahoma, 101
household dysfunction
  adult health risk behaviors related to, 11–14
"humaning"
  described, 8
humanity
  in self-compassion, 123
human needs
  burnout and, 8–11
  types of, 9–11
hygiene
  sleep. *see* sleep hygiene
hyperfreeze
  described, 140
hypofreeze
  described, 140

ICD-11. *see* International Classification of Diseases, Eleventh Revision (ICD-11)
identifying/appreciating your own social, cultural, and psychological risks, 3–31
  activities for, 16–29. *see also specific types and* identifying/appreciating your own social, cultural, and psychological risks activities
  discovering, 14–16
  evaluate/plan for use, 29
  final thoughts, 30–31
  introduction, 3–8
  theory/background, 8–14
identifying/appreciating your own social, cultural, and psychological risks activities, 16–29
  Adverse Childhood Experience Questionnaire for Adults, 23–27
  Burnout Risk-Factor Checklist, 17–21
  Inventory of Toxic Cultural Values activity, 27–29
  The Story of Grind Culture in My Family activity, 21–23
integration
  brain. *see* brain integration
internal experiences
  naming of, 88–90. *see also* Name It to Tame It activity

INDEX

International Classification of Diseases, Eleventh Revision (ICD-11) of WHO, 37, 38*f*
interpersonal relationships
  burnout related to, 14–16
intersectionality
  burnout-related, xxviii–xxix
  defined, xxviii
  described, xxviii–xxix
Inventory of Toxic Cultural Values activity, 27–29
  goal, 27
  instructions, 27–29
Isoard-Gautheur, S., 93–94
isolation
  burnout due to, 11

Jackson, S. E., 36, 38*f*
Johnson, S., 137
Joinson, C., 38*f*
Jones, K., 27–28
journaling
  Burnout Risk-Factor Checklist–related, 20–21
joyful movement
  described, 91–92
  safety from, 92–93
Joyful Movement and Exercise activity, 90–93
  goal, 91
  instructions, 91–93

Kaiser Permanente
  on links between adult health risk behaviors and childhood abuse/household dysfunction, 11–14
Keltner, D., 160, 166–67
  "eight wonders of life" of, 166–67
Kincaid, G., 85
kindness
  in self-compassion, 122
Kirby, R., 162

layer(s)
  stressors as, 7
learning when/how to slow down, step back, and walk away, 59–77
  activities for, 66–75. *see also specific types and* learning when/how to slow down, step back, and walk away activities
  evaluate/plan for use, 75

final thoughts, 76–77
introduction, 59–61
theory/background, 61–63
learning when/how to slow down, step back, and walk away activities
  Big Breaks and Little Rests activity, 68–70
  Discernment–When to Walk Away activity, 72–75
  Healthy Mind Platter activity, 66–68
  Sleep Hygiene Checklist, 70–72
"Lending a Hand: Social Regulation of the Neural Response to Threat," 139
Leverage Your Power and Privilege activity, 167–70
  goal, 168
  instructions, 168–70
life
  unexpected factors in, 175–76
loneliness
  burnout related to, 14–16
Lorde, A., 93, 171
Louv, R., 166
Love Sense: The Revolutionary New Science of Romantic Relationships, 137

Madanes, C., 8–9
Man's Search for Meaning, 159–60
Maslach Burnout Inventory–General Survey (MBI-GS), 42
Maslach Burnout Inventory (MBI), 36–37
Maslach Burnout Inventory (MBI) activity, 42–44
  factors associated with, 42–44
  goal, 42
  instructions, 42–44
Maslach, C., 36, 38*f*
mastery
  in renewal/recovery from burnout, 93
Maté, G., 79–80
Mayo Clinic
  on burnout, 38*f*
MBI. *see* Maslach Burnout Inventory (MBI)
MBI-GS. *see* Maslach Burnout Inventory–General Survey (MBI-GS)
McKee-Lopez, G., 13
meaning
  what generates, 158
medical diagnoses
  burnout associated with, 6
Melamed, S., 62

Menakem, R., 27, 146
mental load
　described, 82–84
　research-based impacts of carrying, 83–84
mindfulness
　in self-compassion, 123
monitor
　in brain, 121–22, 124
motivation
　brain science behind, 121–22
movement
　joyful. *see* joyful movement
My Burnout Danger Rating activity, 47–53, 48*f*
　behaviors/symptoms, 50
　emotions/feelings, 51
　goal, 47
　instructions, 47–52, 48*f*
　physical sensations/symptoms, 51–52
　risk-level warning sign, 47–49, 48*f*
My Capital-P Purpose activity, 162–63
　goal, 163
　instructions, 163

Nagoski, A., xxi
Nagoski, E., xxi, 120, 121, 124, 141, 151
"name it to tame it," 15
Name It to Tame It activity, 88–90
　goal, 88
　instructions, 88–90
"Nap Bishop," 63–64
Nap Ministry, xxvii, 63–64
National Public Radio, 170
natural settings
　spending time in, xxi–xxii
need(s)
　human. *see* human needs
Neff, K., 120–22, 127
"no"
　practicing saying, 63
Nontoxic Gratitude activity, 129–30
　goal, 129
　instructions, 129–30

Obama, B., 47
Okun, T., 27–28
Option B: Facing Adversity, Building Resilience, and Finding Joy, 101
Original ACE Checklist, 24–25
Oxford English Dictionary
　on gratitude, 129

Pace, D., 79, 96
parasympathetic nervous system, 81
parent(s)
　burnout among, 6–7
Parental Burnout Assessment, 21
Parker, D., 116
Parton, D., 44
Patrick-Goudreau, C., 135
perfectionism
　burnout related to, 9
persevering
　perspectives on, 159–60
personal power
　perspectives on, 159–60
Petersen, A. H., 3, 157
Philadelphia ACE Survey, 24, 25
physical sensations
　in recognizing when you are careening toward burnout, 51–52
political factors
　burnout related to, 14–16
Polyvagal Ladder
　Dana's, 102, 103*f*
Polyvagal Theory, 102
Polyvagal Theory in Therapy: Engaging the Rhythm of Regulation, 100, 102, 103*f*
Porges, S.W., 102
"positive dependency," 138
positivity
　activities related to, 108–15. *see also specific types and* figuring out what keeps your fire going activities
　helpful, 105–6
　toxic. *see* toxic positivity
power
　burnout and, 5, 8
　described, 5
　leveraging of, 167–70. *see also* Leverage Your Power and Privilege activity
　personal. *see* personal power
pressure-release valves
　cultivating healthy, 135–56. *see also* cultivating healthy pressure-release valves
privilege
　burnout and, 5, 8
　described, 5
　leveraging of, 167–70. *see also* Leverage Your Power and Privilege activity

INDEX

processing
  described, 26–27
Professional Quality of Life Measure (Pro-QOL), 38f
ProQOL. *see* Professional Quality of Life Measure (ProQOL)
psychological risks
  identifying/appreciating one's own, 3–31. *see also* identifying/appreciating your own social, cultural, and psychological risks
purpose
  what generates, 158

quest(s)
  defined, 69

Raymaker, D. M., 41
Recognize Your "Core-Self" Energy activity, 44–46
  goal, 44
  instructions, 44–46
recognizing when you are careening toward burnout, 33–57
  activities for, 42–55. *see also specific types and* recognizing when you are careening toward burnout activities
  discovering, 39–41
  evaluate/plan for use, 55–56
  final thoughts, 56–57
  introduction, 33–35
  theory/background, 33–37, 38f
recognizing when you are careening toward burnout activities
  Accountability Partners activity, 53–55
  MBI activity, 42–44. *see also* Maslach Burnout Inventory (MBI) activity
  My Burnout Danger Rating activity, 47–53, 48f
  Recognize Your "Core-Self" Energy activity, 44–46
  Reconnect With What Lights You Up activity, 113–15
  goal, 114
  instructions, 114–15
recovery
  burnout-related. *see* burnout recovery
relatedness
  in renewal/recovery from burnout, 94
relation
  bodies in, 137–39

"Relational Activity Add-Ons"
  described, xxiv–xxv
relationship(s)
  healthy. *see* healthy relationships
  interpersonal. *see* interpersonal relationships
  safety in, 137
relaxation
  in renewal/recovery from burnout, 93
"releasing stress," 142
resilience
  building of, 101–2
  described, 101–2
  theory/background on, 101–6, 103f
Rest Is Resistance, xxvii, 63–64
Richelson, G., 36, 38f
risk(s). *see specific types, e.g.,* psychological risks
risk-level warning sign
  burnout-related, 47–49, 48f
Rock, D., 88
Rosen, D., 70–71
Roskam, I., 21
Rothschild, B., xiii–xv, 121, 123, 131

Saad, L. F., 167
sabbaticals
  types of, 69
safe coping strategies, 136
safety
  joyful movement and, 92–93
  in relationships, 137
Salzberg, S., 33
SAMHSA. *see* Substance Abuse and Mental Health Services Administration (SAMHSA)
Sandberg, S., 101
sandwich generation
  defined, 6
Sarrazin, P., 93–94
Schabram, K., 61–62, 68–69
Schwartz, R., 44–46, 109
self
  core. *see* core-self
  "Eight C's of Self," 44–46
self-awareness
  burnout impact on, 33
self-care
  burnout and, xix–xx
self-compassion
  components of, 122–23

self-compassion (*continued*)
    defined, 15
    exercises in achieving, 127–28
    in throwing your hands up without giving up, 122–23
self-compassion process, 122
Self-Compassion–Self-Confidence activity, 127–28
    goal, 127
    instructions, 127–28
sensation(s)
    physical. *see* physical sensations
sense of accomplishment
    decreased, 36
sense of isolation
    burnout due to, 11
Seven Ways to Complete the Stress-Response Cycle activity, 85–87
    goal, 86
    instructions, 86–87
Siegel, D. J., 15, 66–68, 88
significance
    as human need, 9
    what generates, 158
"simple" things become big things
    burnout and, 5–6
sleep deficit
    burnout related to, 62–63
sleep hygiene
    described, 62
Sleep Hygiene Checklist, 70–72
    goal, 70
    instructions, 70–72
slow down
    learning when/how to, 59–77. *see also* learning when/how to slow down, step back, and walk away
social risks
    identifying/appreciating one's own, 3–31. *see also* identifying/appreciating your own social, cultural, and psychological risks
social support
    in burnout prevention, 10–11
    as human need, 10
sociocultural factors
    burnout related to, 14–16
Solomon, M., 138
something bigger
    focusing on, 157–73. *see also* focusing on something bigger

Something to Look Forward to activity, 108–9
    goal, 108
    instructions, 108–9
sonder
    described, 160
spiritual bypassing, 105
Stamm, B. H., 38*f*
Steinem, G., 108
step back
    learning when/how to, 59–77. *see also* learning when/how to slow down, step back, and walk away
stress
    burnout-related, 79–97. *see also* doing something with the stress
    caregiver, 35
    defined, 79–80
    doing something with, 79–97. *see also* doing something with the stress
    "releasing," 142
    relief from, 85–95. *see also specific types and* doing something with the stress activities
stress management
    described, 79
stressor(s)
    as layers, 7
stress-reducing conversation, 149–51. *see also* The Stress-Reducing Conversation activity
    guidelines for, 150–51
stress relief activities, 85–95. *see also specific types and* doing something with the stress activities
stress-response cycle
    described, 81–82
    seven ways to complete, 85–87. *see also* Seven Ways to Complete the Stress-Response Cycle activity
Stress Risk-Factor Checklist, 17–21. *see also* Burnout Risk-Factor Checklist
submit
    described, 139
Substance Abuse and Mental Health Services Administration (SAMHSA), 52–53
substance use
    as problematic, 52–53
Suni, E., 70–71
sympathetic nervous system, 81

INDEX

TapRoot, 164
Tawwab, N. G., 149
The Power of Attachment: How to Create Deep and Lasting Intimate Relationships, 137–38
The Story of Grind Culture in My Family activity, 21–23
    goal, 21–22
    instructions, 22–23
The Stress-Reducing Conversation activity, 149–51
    goal, 149
    instructions, 150–51
thriving
    burnout vs., xix
    described, xix
throwing your hands up without giving up, 119–34
    activities for, 126–32. *see also specific types and* throwing your hands up without giving up activities
    burnout vs., 119–34
    discovering, 123–25
    empathy dial in, 123
    evaluate/plan for use, 132–33
    final thoughts, 133–34
    introduction, 119–20
    monitoring in, 121–22, 124
    self-compassion in, 122–23
    theory/background, 120–23
throwing your hands up without giving up activities, 126–32
    Figure Out Your Empathy Dial activity, 130–32
    Nontoxic Gratitude activity, 129–30
    Self-Compassion–Self-Confidence activity, 127–28
    Work With Your Brain to Reduce Frustration activity, 126–27
tired
    types of, 175
Toker, S., 62
toxic cultural values, 27–28. *see also* Inventory of Toxic Cultural Values activity
toxic positivity
    burnout and, xxii
    defined, 109
    described, 104
    examples of, 110
    helpful positivity vs., 105–6
    phrases that uninvite, 110–11
    theory/background on, 101–6, 103*f*
Toxic Positivity: Keeping It Real in a World Obsessed With Being Happy, 105–6
toxic positivity phrases, 104–5
trigger(s)
    defined, 113
    examples of, 113
    glimmers vs., 100–1
Turning Into the Skid activity, 146–49
    goal, 146
    instructions, 147–49
"turn into the skid"
    described, 146

Un-Becoming Comfortably Numb activity, 144–45
    goal, 144
    instructions, 144–45
unexpected factors in life, 175–76
University of Chicago
    Center for Cognitive and Social Neuroscience at, 138
University of Oklahoma
    Hope Research Center at, 101

Valerio, N., 23
value(s)
    core, 164–66
    cultural. *see* cultural values
    types of, 164–65
valve(s)
    pressure-release, 135–56. *see also* cultivating healthy pressure-release valves; pressure-release valves
variety
    as human need, 9

Wagner, K. E., 53
walk away
    learning when/how to, 59–77. *see also* learning when/how to slow down, step back, and walk away
Welwood, J., 105
"What Does Burnout Feel Like?"
    common responses to, 39–40
"What's mentionable is manageable," 15
WHO. *see* World Health Organization (WHO)
Winfrey, O., 42
wishing
    described, 101

wishing (*continued*)
  hope vs., 101
work environment
  burnout impact on, xxvi
working holidays
  defined, 69
working parents
  burnout among, 6–7

Work With Your Brain to Reduce Frustration activity, 126–27
  goal, 126
  instructions, 126–27
World Health Organization (WHO)
  ICD-11 of, 37, 38*f*

Zuckerman, J., 104

The 8 Keys to Mental Health Series
Babette Rothschild, Series Editor

This book series provides readers with brief, high-quality self-help books on a variety of topics in mental health. Filled with exercises and practical strategies, these paperbacks empower readers to help themselves.

Learn more about all books in the series at **wwnorton.com/8keysseries**

8 Keys to Brain-Body Balance by Robert Scaer
978-0-393-70747-2 • 176 pages • $21.95

8 Keys to Building Your Best Relationships by Daniel A. Hughes
978-0-393-70820-2 • 208 pages • $19.95

8 Keys to Eliminating Passive-Aggressiveness by Andrea Brandt
978-0-393-70846-2 • 224 pages • $23.99

8 Keys to End Bullying: Strategies for Parents & Schools
by Signe Whitson
978-0-393-70928-5 • 240 pages • $19.95

8 Keys to End Emotional Eating by Howard S. Farkas
978-0-393-71232-2 • 200 pages • $19.95

8 Keys to Forgiveness by Robert Enright
978-0-393-73405-8 • 256 pages • $19.95

8 Keys to Healing, Managing, and Preventing Burnout
by Morgan Johnson
978-1-324-05388-0 • 224 pages • $24.99

8 Keys to Mental Health Through Exercise by Christina G. Hibbert
978-0-393-71122-6 • 304 pages • $19.95

8 Keys to Parenting Children with ADHD by Cindy Goldrich
978-0-393-71067-0 • 240 pages • $23.95

8 Keys to Practicing Mindfulness: Practical Strategies for Emotional Health and Well-Being by Manuela Mischke-Reeds
978-0-393-70795-3 • 256 pages • $19.95

8 Keys to Raising the Quirky Child: How to Help a Kid Who Doesn't (Quite) Fit In by Mark Bowers
978-0-393-70920-9 • 320 pages • $19.95

8 Keys to Recovery from an Eating Disorder: Effective Strategies from Therapeutic Practice and Personal Experience by Carolyn Costin and Gwen Schubert Grabb
978-0-393-70695-6 • 296 pages • $28.99

8 Keys to Recovery from an Eating Disorder Workbook by Carolyn Costin and Gwen Schubert Grabb
978-0-393-71128-8 • 288 pages • $28.99

8 Keys to Safe Trauma Recovery: Take-Charge Strategies to Empower Your Healing by Babette Rothschild
978-0-393-70605-5 • 192 pages • $25.99

8 Keys to Safe Trauma Recovery Workbook by Babette Rothschild and Vanessa Bear
978-1-324-02012-7 • 328 pages • $26.99

8 Keys to Stress Management by Elizabeth Anne Scott
978-0-393-70809-7 • 224 pages • $19.95

prices are in USD and subject to change